T0104473

# Demons Nephilim Angels

## The World That Then Was

ETIENNE M. GRAVES JR.

Order this book online at www.trafford.com
or email orders@trafford.com

Most Trafford titles are also available at major online book retailers.

Bible Citation:
The Companion Bible: King James Version (KJV), © 1922, 2011,
Kregel Publications. All rights reserved.

Printed in the United States of America.

ISBN: 978-1-4907-3173-5 (sc)
ISBN: 978-1-4907-3175-9 (hc)
ISBN: 978-1-4907-3174-2 (e)

Library of Congress Control Number: 2014905506

*Trafford rev. 03/26/2014*

 www.trafford.com

North America & international
toll-free: 1 888 232 4444 (USA & Canada)
fax: 812 355 4082

# Contents

# PREFACE

In 1999 I had a dream. In this dream, I was lying down on a sandy hill. As I sat up, I looked up and saw a huge black ball in the sky. It looked like planet Earth. I saw what looked like a man walking on top of the Earth covered in pitch-black darkness. He had his hands stretched out in front of him like he was a zombie walking to the edge of the Earth. I called out to him, "Turn around, go back. You are going to fall!" But it seemed as though he could not hear me. When he got to the end, he fell, and I could see and feel the thud when he hit the ground. There was something that was controlling him. I looked up again, and I saw the black Earth covered in darkness full of people. It was as if they were in some sort of trance, and under a spell of deception. I screamed at the top of my lungs, "Turn around, you're going to fall. Go the other way!" But it was to no avail because they all fell. I could faintly see that there was something swaying and pulling them toward their death. I asked myself, "Why couldn't they see or hear me? Who or what is deceiving them, luring or drawing them to their apparent death? Why was I watching it? Why were they in a trance?" Eventually, the ball turned into the people walking on top of the Earth, pushing and shoving their way to get to the end. It seemed as though on their way down, they snapped out of it, but by then it was too late. What did God want me to do to turn these people around? I asked God that question, and He started me on this journey towards the truth and this quest to teach the hidden information because we are living in the last days. I did my best to draw my dream. I am by no means an artist, but Isaiah 60:1-3 will help explain my dream.

> Arise (awake), shine . . . . Behold, the darkness shall cover the earth, and gross (drop down) darkness on the people: but the Lord shall arise upon thee and His glory shall be seen upon thee. And the Gentiles shall come to thy light and kings to the brightness of thy rising.

God is telling all of us to wake up so that the glory of God can cover and protect us from the coming darkness of deception. The only way for that to happen is to walk in the truth about the Word of God. As you can see in my dream, darkness was covering the Earth just as it did in Isaiah 60:2. It says that *gross darkness shall cover the people.* The word *gross* means to drop down. The people in the dream were dropping down to their death because they didn't know the truth.

My job is to teach people the truth so that they come out of darkness (death, sorrow, misery, and deception) into His marvelous light. God will draw people who will seek the light that leads to the truth to MEMO.

Darkness can hold people in captivity, but God's word is a lamp to guide us and a light for our path for us to follow. The explanation of my teachings will give light and bring wisdom to those who don't want to be ignorant about God's word anymore.

*The entrance of thy (God's) word will bring light* (Pss. 119:105, 130). When God's word comes in, it eradicates all darkness. Here's a drawing of my dream below of people on the earth walking in a prison of darkness.

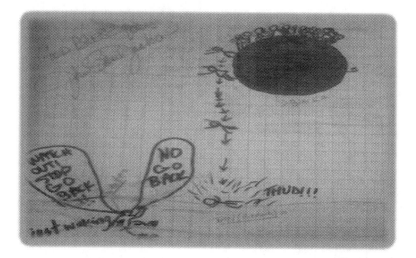

# INTRODUCTION

The Bible teaches us what happened with the rise and fall of celestial beings and demons, but this subject is so infrequently mentioned in the pulpit that God has called and given me, Etienne M. Graves Jr., founder of Melchizedek's Excellent Ministry Order (MEMO), information to give to His children and others. This subject is as important as it is fascinating. God gave Daniel a prophecy of the end time. He told Daniel to shut up the words and seal the book until the time of the end, *when many shall run to and fro and knowledge shall increase* because we have the technological tools to receive more globally updated information from the Internet via computers.

Knowledge is no longer sealed up. It is revealed through revelation knowledge by the Holy Spirit and the Bible, the Word of God. As I read my Bible to study, I ask the Holy Spirit to teach me what the Word of God is saying. According to John 14:26, "But the

Comforter, which is the Holy Ghost, whom the Father will send in my name, He shall teach you all things, and bring all things to your remembrance, whatsoever I have said unto you." To learn more about the Bible, we must diligently seek the truth. He rewards those who diligently seek Him and His truth.

Many of us Christians won't get the truth because most of us are just reading the Bible or using audiobooks, iPads, iPhones, and DVDs instead of studying, and doing research by looking up the etymology of the words in Hebrew and Greek and running references on the scriptures to see how the scriptures connect. Our Heavenly Father told us in 2 Timothy 2:15 to study (use our mind to gain knowledge to learn more about the Bible). Work hard so God can say, "Well done!" Be a good worker, one who does not need to be ashamed when God examines your work. We allow pastors, teachers, and others to interpret the Bible for us, and we just take their word that what they are saying is true. When you don't study, you are destroyed or deceived for lack of revelation knowledge (Hosea 4:6).

MEMO (Melchizedek's Excellent Ministry Order) is here for you to see the truth, hear the truth, know the truth, and hopefully live the truth without being deceived. Then the truth will make you free. Let's put aside old traditional fables about the Bible and your inflated ego and foolish pride, which won't allow you to receive or even consider the truth. Many Christians have gotten so far from the truth that they believe the lies carry more credibility. Then they take for granted that the lies about the Bible must be the truth.

"As newborn babes, desire the sincere milk of the word, that ye may grow thereby" (1 Pet. 2:2). As a baby in Christ, we were fed "with milk and not with meat: for hitherto ye were not able to bear it, neither yet now are ye able" (1 Cor. 3:2).

We are supposed to grow up and mature so that we can digest the meat of the word like mature adults or mature Christians.

As a full-grown Christian, you should be able to teach others, but some of us still need someone to teach us again and again with the very first principles that we learned as a baby Christian about God's word. Some don't want to let go of the baby bottle or the pacifier. It's time for some solid food, like meat. For everyone who partakes only of milk is not accustomed to the word of righteousness for he is an infant. But solid food is for the mature, one who because of practice have their senses trained to discern good and evil or right and wrong teaching (Heb. 5:12-14).

So put down the baby bottle, pacifier, and baby food and start to eat some solid food, like meat or chicken. You should be very hungry for the truth by now. To digest solid food, we must go back to the beginning of everything in the book of Genesis, because if you don't understand Genesis, you will never understand the end of everything in the book of Revelation. Try not to close your mind to the information that I'll be sharing in this book, because when you close your mind, you close the door to the opportunity for you to receive the truth about God's word. Whether you agree or disagree, ask the Holy Spirit to guide you, because according to John 16:13, "Howbeit when He, the Spirit of truth, is come, He will guide you into all truth: for He shall not speak of Himself: but whatsoever He shall hear, that shall He speak; and He will shew you things to come." The Holy Spirit is the ultimate teacher, and His job is to teach us about things in the past, present, future, and about this world that we live in. The Bible teaches us about the previous ancient worlds that then were.

# PART 1

# The World That Then Was

Whereby _the world that then_ was, being overflowed with
water, perished [destroyed]: But the heavens and the earth,
which _are now_, by the same word are kept in store, reserved
unto the fire against the day of judgment and perdition of
ungodly men. (2 Pet. 3:6, 7)

Peter tells us that there was another world age before the age
that we live in. The world that existed eons ago was destroyed by
water. We have fossils and relics that prove that there was another
world before this world that we live in was created. A lot of people
are living in darkness. Moses tells us in Genesis about what
happened on planet Earth.

# 1

## *In the Beginning God . . .*

What really happened in the beginning? And why has this truth been hidden for so long? To find out the truth, we must go back to the beginning of everything in the book of Genesis.

*In the beginning God created the heaven and the earth. (Gen. 1:1)*

In the Beginning God is a spiritual personification or a Person. When we read this scripture, we interpret it as time and not as an entity. In John 1:1, it states, *"In the beginning was the word and the word was with God and the word [logos] was God."* The fact that it states in the beginning *was God*, not *is God*, implies a continued action, meaning He was already preexistent. God exists outside of time but in eternity. The logos is the energy or the speech of God in (human) form, but God could appear in any form (Job 38:1, 42:5; Gen. 12:7, 17:1, 26:2, 24). The words *Jesus was with God* means all that He said, did, and showed pointed to the Father.

Isaiah 48:3 reads, *"I have declared the <u>former things from the beginning</u>; and they went forth <u>out of my mouth</u>, and I shewed them; I did them suddenly, and they came to pass."*

So In the Beginning God (the word), created the heavens and the earth. Everything was made good, but something happened to make the earth without form, an empty waste, and darkness was upon the face of the very great deep.

Deep in Hebrew in *Strong's Exhaustive Concordance of the Bible* is an abyss (tehom-tehhome), a surging mass of water that was agitated greatly.

*And the earth <u>was</u> [became] without <u>form</u> [waste, confusion], and void [empty]; and darkness [misery, death] was upon the face of the deep. And the Spirit of God [Holy Ghost] moved upon the face of the waters. (Gen. 1:2)*

*And the Spirit of God moved upon the "face of the waters."* The word *moved* in Hebrew is rachaph (raw-khaf), which means to brood. Brooding is like a hen sitting on her eggs to keep them warm, protect them, and lead them out of darkness. God was preparing a special place for His children that are made in His image and was protecting His DNA from something or someone. DNA abides in a matrix of water. The fact that DNA is in water is the primary reason why it has it's helix ladder shape (as you will see later).

The Holy Ghost was covering by brooding over the face of the waters. How long ago did all this take place? How long ago is the beginning? Well, no one really knows because we cannot date

God. He has no beginning and no end. Did God create the earth that way?

According to Isaiah 45:18, "*For thus saith the Lord that created the heavens; God Himself that formed the earth and made it; He hath established it, He created it not in vain, He formed it to be inhabited: I am the Lord and there is none else.*"

*God made the earth for a purpose and for it to be occupied.* In Genesis 1:9, it states, "Let the dry [confused, ashamed] land appear:" and it was so." The word *was* in verse 2 should read *became,* so the earth became an empty waste of misery and death.

What or who caused the earth to be an uninhabited, worthless waste and in darkness since He didn't create it that way? How did it turn into chaos (extreme confusion or disorder)? Why was the dry land ashamed? Something happened. God was angry at someone or about something. To find out, we must go to Isaiah for some answers and learn about Lucifer and what he did to anger God.

There were three worlds (ages). There was the world (anion-age), the original earth, the chaotic earth, and the restored earth from Genesis 1:3 and forward. What happened that turned the original earth into the chaotic earth? In Isaiah 14:12, this statement is made by God, "How art thou fallen from heaven O, *Lucifer* son of the morning!"

You can see by the exclamation point (!) that this is a statement and not a question. The original Hebrew makes it clear that the word *Lucifer* really is not an accurate translation. *Light bringer* or *bearer* isn't what was intended in this passage. *Lucifer* is a Latin word, and sadly, the phrase translated is misleading. It should have been translated *O shining star* instead of *Lucifer.*

*Lucifer* in Hebrew is *heylel* (hay-lael), in the sense of brightness as the morning star. The actual Hebrew word *hay-lael* does not mean *"star"* but *"bright or clear sounding,"* as in singing *hallelujah/ allelujah.* Although it really means *brightly colored or shining* and, appropriately, *boastfulness and pride,* the next phrase, *"son of the morning"* or *morning star,* should actually read *"son of the dawning,"* as in the earliest or the first God created. *Son* in Hebrew is *Ben* (bane); a *son*, as a builder of the family name and morning, is *shachar* (shakhar), dawn or early.

God created the Angels at the dawn of all His creation. A more precise translation from the Hebrew should read, "O, clear sounding, bright shining, and boasting son from the beginning." I refer to him as *Heylael Ben Shachar* (Lucifer), who was trying to be God and wanted to be used in His place.

*"I Jesus have sent mine angel to testify unto you these things in the churches. I am the root and the offspring of David, and the Bright and Morning Star" (Rev. 22:16).*

Jesus is the Bright and Morning Star, not Heylael. Heylael is "the anointed cherub that covers." What was he covering?

# 2

## *The <u>Anointed Cherub</u> that Covers*

L et's find out more about this being and what his purpose was and the exact reason why he was created. Let's go to Ezekiel 28:12-18.

*Son of man, take up a <u>lamentation</u> [strike a musical note, chant or wail at a funeral] upon the king of <u>Tyrus</u>, and say unto him, Thus saith the Lord God, Thou sealest up the sum, full of wisdom, and perfect in beauty.* (verse 12)

*Thou hast been in <u>Eden</u> [paradise] the garden of God; every <u>precious</u> [valuable] stone was thy <u>covering</u> [entwined decoration], the sardius, topaz, and the diamond, the beryl, the onyx, and the jasper, the sapphire, the emerald, and the carbuncle, and gold: the* *workmanship [ministry, employment], of thy tabrets [to drum, a tambourine] and of thy pipes [bezels, flutes] was prepared [set up, fixed] in thee in the day that thou wast created.* (verse 13)

*Thou art the anointed [expansion, outstretched wings, to paint or rub on ] cherub that covereth; and I have set thee so: thou wast upon the holy mountain of God; thou hast walked up and down in the midst of the stones of fire.* (verse 14)

Pay close attention to the tenses of the verbs; *to walk* and *to be* are past tense. He no longer is walking or in the holy mountain, but he is still the anointed cherub that covers.

*Thou wast perfect in thy ways from the day that thou wast created, till iniquity was found in thee.* (verse 15)

*By the multitude of thy merchandise [trade, to travel for trading] they have filled the midst of thee with violence [wrong, unjust gain, cruelty], and thou hast sinned: therefore I will cast thee as profane out of the mountain of God: and I will destroy [to wander away, to perish] thee, O covering cherub, from the midst of the stones of fire.* (verse 16)

*Once again, it is present tense, "covering cherub".*

*Thine heart was lifted up because of thy beauty [to be bright, beautiful], thou hast corrupted [to decay, to will it] thy wisdom [skillful, which, wise, teach] by reason of thy brightness [to shine, splendor, beauty, be light]: I will cast thee to the ground, I will lay thee before kings, that they may behold thee.* (verse 17)

*Thou hast defiled [pollute] sanctuaries [sacred places, temple] by the multitude of thine iniquities [perverse, depraved], by the iniquity of thy trafflick; therefore will I bring forth a fire from the midst of thee, it shall devour thee, and I will bring thee to ashes upon the earth in the sight of all them that behold thee.* (verse 18)

I have underlined some key phrases so that we can break it down and explain the truth about this cherub. To break it down, I got help from the Holy Spirit, revelation knowledge, and from *Strong's Exhaustive Concordance of the Bible* because it's a dictionary of the Hebrew and Greek words that were translated from the King James Version (KJV).

The King James Bible is the only definitive version because it is the only version that matches up with prophecies, the symbols, and understanding of what really happened in the ancient world. There is far more information in the original KJV than any other translated versions of the Bible, and it has not been changed or added to.

First of all, it is interesting to note that our body is composed of water and many of the same mineral elements that are found in some of the stones that adorned Heylael, primarily carbon, which is found in diamonds. Notice that he was created perfect in beauty and full of wisdom.

He was in Eden, but he was not a snake. He was a shining one as you see from this description. He had nine precious gemstones, and gold were placed in him on the day he was created. Heylael, the cherub, was adorned and decorated with an array of gems. These gems were encased in gold on his outstretched wings that formed an arch similar to the rainbow that you see after it rains. His wings were like a transparent rainbow that glittered with the light from God. Many of these stones are the same colors that are found in the rainbow in the record of Noah's life.

God's covenant with Noah declared that He would never again destroy the earth with a flood in Genesis 9:8-17. The rainbow in the clouds is a covenant sign from God to humans that He would never again destroy the world with water.

There is an emerald rainbow surrounding the throne of God. Emerald represents life and healing, and because trees and plants are alive, they are used to make medicines to help heal our bodies.

Ezekiel compares the glory of God to that of a rainbow in Ezekiel 1:28. This anointed cherub, this beautiful magnificent creature, had something to do with the throne of God and His glory.

Heylael's covering was like a prism shooting out, flashing streams of beautiful colors like the rainbow. He illuminated the light of God. This is where the term *Illuminati* originated from. (See chapter 9 for more information about the Illuminati.)

"God is Light, a Spirit, and a Consuming [blazing] fire" (1 John 1:5, Heb. 12:29, and Exod. 24:17). God is light (dunamis-energy, power). His dunamis or dynamite power is so powerful like that of a fire that He has to veil, clothe, and wrap Himself in light (Ps. 104:2).

Heylael believed he was special because he was illuminated by the light of God. He would go into the presence of God and absorb all of God's Shekinah Glory in Heaven into his jewels and then go out into the outer courts and reflect, refract, and magnify the glory of God to those living on the earth and on the planets. It is similar to the way a diamond disperses light and glistens when light hits it.

The Angels would see God's image in the jewels and bow down to the image of God being portrayed, proclaiming, "Halel-u-Jah!" meaning *you are Jah*! Praise Jah, the Lord! They were not bowing down to him but to the image of the Almighty God.

He was able to manipulate and control light and alter images. He wore nine stones, just like there are nine gifts of the Holy Spirit and nine fruits of the spirit. The number 9 represents harvest or birth or fruit. So he was skilled in harvesting or birthing things and bringing forth fruit. But what kind of fruit?

You know what kind of tree it is by the fruit that it produces. This cherub was producing rotten fruit.

This cherub was perfect in wisdom and beauty. He was anointed. He had the power of the Holy Spirit smeared on his covering. These same stones are seen in Exodus 28:9-14 when referring to Aaron, the brother of Moses, the first official high priest of Israel.

The high priest functioned as a mediator between the children of Israel and God. He was the go-between for heaven and earth. Aaron wore twelve stones to represent the twelve tribes of Israel, and the number 12 represents union and government. Without union with God, he was not supposed to govern.

What about the rest of his body? He had tambourines and flutes embedded in his body. In Isaiah 14, it says he had viols or strings for strumming, like on a harp, violin, or guitar. He was anointed, set apart for a specific purpose, the same way that all of us are created for a specific purpose by the Beginning God.

Part of his ministry was to be a walking praise instrument to God. When he walked, the tambourine played. His heartbeat was like a drumbeat. His body was punctured with flutes that played like an accordion (organ). We breathe air. He breathes music. He led the praise and worship for the terrestrial and celestial beings and Angels on the planets and in heaven. Heylael had percussion instruments built into his very being. When he played music, lights, sounds, and colors in a harmonious, melodious, and reverential symphony reflected God's glory. These beings worshiped God, and this cherub thought that all of this worship and praise should have been for him. The other Angels couldn't go into God's presence like he could. He was privileged to be a representative of the image of God. He covered the mercy seat in heaven. In other words, in order to get to God, you had to go through Heylael.

The Bible says that he was an anointed cherub. What exactly is a cherub? One thing for sure, a cherub is not the pictures of any of those Caucasian babies with wings. Those are not cherubs.

Cherubs are somewhat different from Angels. They are a celestial order of beings distinguished from the Angels. Angels are created spirits used as messengers. Cherubs are not dismissed on errands as Angels are and are never seen apart from the throne of God. The Bible describes a cherub as a creature having the following:

- *Four faces and four wings*
- *The face of an ox, a man, a lion, and an eagle*
- *The likeness of a man*
- *Hands of a man*
- *Straight legs and calves or hooves, the appearance of light bright coals of fire*
- *The appearance of lamps, bright fire and flashing lightning going up and down their bodies*
- *Rings (backs) are full of dreadful eyes*
- *Reflecting the glory of God*
- *Guarding the throne of God*
- *They go where the spirit goes (Ezek. 1:10)*

I want you to observe the fact that a cherub looks like a man and has hands like a man. So Ezekiel is referring to a man in verse 28. He is talking about a man or a living creature because that's what a cherub is. Earlier in this chapter God refers to the prince of Tyrus as a man and not God. In Isaiah 14:16, it states, "is this the man that made the earth to tremble, that did shake kingdoms?" In Mark 8:33, Jesus rebuked Satan through Peter because Satan savours (interest oneself with) the things of men.

The Bible never mentions Angels with wings, but it does mention cherubim and seraphim with wings. This is where the term *two-faced* comes from because the cherub has two faces on one side and two faces on another side. Notice also that this is one of the reasons why Satan is able to disguise himself in different forms. From this description, he was a mighty, majestic, fearful creature. He had the likeness of a man with four faces: a lion, ox, man, and an eagle with the hands of a man under his wings. Basically, he was a hybrid, part cherub and part man.

Cherubs have eyes all over their bodies and wings. God created man (us) in His image and likeness to replace this cherub/man a.k.a. Heylael. Man's responsibility is to be His high priest and king, to reflect God's glory, and to show His light in the earth to all creation.

Satan/Heylael is jealous of mankind and hates us because we are created in God's image and Satan is not. We are not hybrids, but he is a hybrid. He is similar to a pet or mascot. He is the anointed cherub that _covers_. Let's explore this word _covers_ from Ezekiel 28.

The word _cover_ in Hebrew is sakak (sawkak), which means to entwine as a screen, to fence in, protect, cover, join together, or shut up. This cherub was entwined like the DNA strands. He had the innate ability to work with DNA. Unfortunately he would eventually use this ability to manipulate genes through deception. God had entwined precious gems in him, but he needed to be silenced because of his deception. He is called a dragon, serpent, devil, Satan, a cherub, seraphim, Lucifer, prince of the power of the air, a snake, and Heylael.

In Revelation 12:9, it records, *"And the great dragon was cast out, that old serpent, called the Devil, and Satan, which deceiveth the whole world: he was cast out into the earth, and his angels were cast out with him."*

The dragon is the serpent, and the serpent is the devil. And the devil is Satan. To analyze this serpent, let's go to Isaiah 6:2-4.

*Above it stood the seraphims: each one had six wings; with twain he covered his face, and with twain he covered his feet, and with twain he did fly. And one cried unto another, and said, "Holy, holy holy is the Lord of hosts: the whole earth is full of his glory." At the posts of the door moved at the voice of him they cried, and the house was filled with smoke.*

According to Strong, seraphim are burning, fiery flying serpents.

In the KJV Companion Bible on page 938, seraphim are *"celestial beings, named but unexplained. They used serpents (Numbers 21:6) because of the burning effect produced by them just as the "nacash" was used of a snake because of its shining skin (Numbers 21:9), as well as of the shining one of Genesis 3:1."* The serpent in the garden of Eden was none other than Heylael, himself.

He was God's veil. Just like when a veil is worn by a woman getting married, she is veiled until she is married to her husband. When the veil is lifted, she is <u>joined</u> as one to her spouse. When there is a death or a funeral, usually the widow wears a veil to show that she has been <u>separated</u> from her spouse.

After God cast Heylael out of heaven, God placed a veil over heaven to separate Satan and his kingdom from God and His kingdom. It is interesting that a *nun* and the *Sphinx* appear to be wearing a pulled-back veil as a headdress. Unfortunately, Heylael seems to have a lot of influence over the Catholic faith, the Sphinx, Egypt, and Africa.

*And he will destroy in the mountain the <u>face</u> [of seraphim or cherubim] of the <u>covering</u> [wrap up, veil] <u>cast</u> [blanketed] over all people, and the <u>veil</u> [cast image] that is <u>spread</u> [interweaved] over all nations. (Isa. 25:7)*

*Because of his position and where he is as a seraph/man/cherub, he is able to block the image and glory of God when he is allowed to by us humans.* It states in Exodus 26:31,

> *And thou shall make a vail [veil] of blue, and purple, and scarlet, and fine twined (twist, like DNA strands) linen of cunning work: with cherubims shall it be made.*

Cherubs are important since God instructed Moses to put them on the veil or curtains before the Holy of Holies, where the mercy seat was located in the tabernacle that Moses replicated with the help of the Holy Spirit.

Heylael was a cherub with huge wings that were so enormous that when he spread them, he could cover a whole atmosphere. When we read "that he walked up and down in the midst of the stones of fire," we need to know what the stones of fire are.

The stones of fire are built stones or rocks of fire. God built the planets to reflect the light from Him. I believe that the stones of fire are planets. From an aerial view, the planets can be seen as stones of fire. When you look at a model of our solar system, the planets are colorful stones that revolve around the sun. The earth was turned upside down. Most likely, the planets were lined up like stepping-stones for Heylael to move to and fro and up and down.

Ezekiel 28 is addressed to the King of Tyrus (rock, stone), who *traveled for trafficking* and walked up and down in God's holy, sacred mountain in heaven and on earth and in between the planets. He was the king before the nations of the world. His beauty, power, wisdom, pride, and creative musical ability all went to his head.

In Ezekiel 28:13, we know that Ezekiel is talking about Satan because in verse 13, it says, "Thou hast been in Eden the garden of God." The King of Tyrus, who lived on the earth, wasn't born when the garden of God existed. The only others who were in the Garden of Eden were Adam and Eve and, of course, the devil, who was demoted from a king to a prince of the power of the air.

When the sons of God (Angels) came to present themselves or stand at their assigned station, Satan came also. In Job 1:7, the Lord asked Satan,

*Whence comest thou? Then Satan answered the Lord, and said "From going to and fro in the earth and from walking up and down in it."*

The phrase *walking up and down in the earth* is the same phrase as *walking up and down in the midst of the stones of fire*, which are also planets. This man's (cherub/seraph) ministry was that of a messenger, ambassador, king, prophet, priest, and teacher. Heylael was the high priest of all the <u>sanctuaries </u>on every inhabitable planet. Remember, he had sanctuaries (chapels and temples of Jehovah) that he was to oversee.

When nightclubs first came into fruition, they were first called sanctuaries, designed to <u>*control*</u> your biorhythms with lights and sounds and colors like a prism.

Obviously, before the veil in the temples of Jehovah, there was sin and iniquity because of Satan. They became temples of idols. He was over *Earth, Mars, the Moon, and "<u>Rahab</u>,"* where he led the praise and worship with music and even preached and taught in the sanctuaries.

Heylael was created perfect or complete until all kinds of wickedness was found in him. This man/cherub/seraph had distorted and perverted his kingdom as well as the kingdom of God and all moral righteousness by making, selling, trading, and pedaling by mixing different kinds of <u>DNA</u> of the beings and animals on planets and on earth.

Cruelty, violence, unjust crimes, slavery, immoral behavior, murder, and the perversion of God's image were committed by Heylael, and he must be punished. God had to take him out of His holy mountain and remove him from his position. He turned his world upside down and scattered the inhabitants abroad.

Behold, the Lord maketh the earth empty, and maketh it waste, and turneth it upside down, and scattereth (dispersed) abroad the inhabitants thereof. (Isa. 24:1)

# 3

## *Mystery Planet Rahab*

H eylael's world included Rahab, a planet that was in between Mars and Jupiter.

The Bible teaches us about Rahab as a place as well as a person. Rahab the person can be found in Joshua chapters 2 and 6.

When Joshua succeeded Moses as the leader of the children of Israel, he led them out of the wilderness into Jericho and, eventually, into the land of Canaan.

He sent out two spies to search out all the country of Canaan before they entered it to attack. Rahab, the harlot, lived in Jericho, which was in Canaan where giants (Nephilim) lived.

Rahab received a message from the King of Jericho telling her that he was looking for the men (two spies) that were staying at her house. The 2 spies were sent there by Joshua to see what was going on and the King of Jericho found out about it. She told the king that the men left and that she didn't know where they were, but if he would pursue after them, that he would catch them before they left Jericho. Jericho was the first city that Israel conquered under Joshua, where Rahab lived.

Everywhere in the Bible that talks about Rahab, except when talking about the generations of David, she is called a harlot. (See Joshua 6:25, Hebrews 11:31, and James 2:25.)

I asked the Lord, why was she called a harlot? He told me that it was to distinguish her as a person from Rahab the place. According to Jewish history, Rahab was an innkeeper and a businesswoman. She hid the spies on the rooftop of her house in the stalks of flax.

The flat roofs were used for drying the stalks of flax that were three-or four-feet stems that had previously been soaked in water and laid out on the flat roof to dry. Furthermore, lamp wicks were made out of linseed oil, which came from flax.

Flax was a very popular plant used to make linen and was also used as a food. Making linen was a common household chore (Prov. 31:13). It was used to make linen garments and ephods that the high priest wore in Leviticus 6:10, 1 Samuel 2:18, and Exodus 39. The Hebrew word for flax can also be linked to the Menorah, which represents the 7 Spirits of God.

After Jesus died, His body was wrapped in a clean linen cloth. It was a Jewish custom to wrap their dead in linen cloth with spices to bury them (John 19:40, Luke 24:12, Matt. 27:59, and Mark 15:46). Rahab was probably selling the flax to make money.

Rahab was a priestess of the Canaanite religion and a public prostitute. Her profession was considered by the people among whom she lived as honorable and not disgraceful, as it now is among us. She lived among people without morals and no fear of God.

Rahab was not married nor did she have any children. I believe that she worshipped Baal because he was supposed to be the god who provided fertility, as she was barren. In Joshua 6:25, it states,

> And Joshua saved Rahab the harlot alive, and her father's household, and all that she had; and she dwelleth in Israel even unto this day: because she hid the messengers, which Joshua sent to spy out Jericho.

Joshua doesn't say anything about Rahab having a husband nor children. Apparently, those who lived in her father's household came to Rahab's house to escape death when the Israelites attacked Jericho.

Rahab had heard of the miracles wrought on behalf of Israel and had become convinced that Israel's God was the true God. When she met the spies, she decided, at the risk of her life, to believe in and trust in their God.

Joshua and his men were grateful both for her military information and her protection of the two spies and carefully spared the life of all of Rahab's family when Jericho fell.

The name of Rahab appears in the genealogy of Jesus. She was the wife of Salmon and the mother of Boaz, Ruth's husband. Rahab would have been an ancestor of David and Jesus.

Because of her belief in the true God, her womb was opened. She is listed in the Hall of Faith in Hebrews 11:31. Obviously, God forgave her and delivered her from being a harlot.

There must have been some similarities between the person Rahab and the place Rahab because Rahab the person seemed to have been a very bold, busy, and confident woman.

Another reason that Rahab was called a harlot was because she left the worship of Baal and followed after God Almighty. The Canaanites probably called her a harlot for leaving and forsaking her religious beliefs. She divorced herself from Baal and married God. Idolatry is considered to be spiritual adultery or spiritual fornication.

In the book of Revelation 17:5, it states,

And upon her forehead was a name written MYSTERY (secret), BABYLON THE GREAT, THE MOTHER OF HARLOTS AND ABOMINATIONS OF THE EARTH.

Babylon was the gateway of the gods and the pit from hell of idolatry, where Rahab lived.

Rahab, while living in Canaan, was involved in all kinds of sins until she started to believe in God Almighty. Everything abominable was done in Canaan. That's why God told the Israelites to destroy everyone and get rid of all their belongings. Joshua killed all the people, their animals, and then burned the city to the ground. They only took the silver, gold, and the vessels of brass and iron to be used in the treasury of the house of the Lord.

Rahab and her relatives were the only people who were spared when Joshua attacked Jericho. Rahab and her relatives relocated and went with Joshua and the children of Israel. In Joshua 6:25, the following is stated:

She [Rahab] dwelleth in Israel even unto this day; because she hid the messengers, which Joshua sent to spy out Jericho.

Rahab the place was a planet that was part of our solar system before God destroyed it. According to Strong, *Rahab in Hebrew* means arrogant, raging, turbulent, afflicter, and a bully, which are all character flaws that describe Satan after his fall from heaven.

Before the creation of Adam, the civilizations of Angels and terrestrial beings existed on the terrestrial planets. Throughout scripture, there is a consistent reference to the first dwelling places of some of the ancient sons of God. These Angels or terrestrial beings created habitations on the stones of fire (planets) for all civilizations and all the host of Heaven to give glory to God the Creator.

On Rahab, which is also called Planet X or Niburu, Heylael had a mansion, throne, or a dwelling place. This planet was a crowded, thriving fortress, probably much like the Earth is now. The people were busy, and there was a lot of activity. It was a nation that had turned lukewarm toward God, their Creator. They sought to break away and liberate themselves away from their Creator and have their own freedom under Heylael.

I believe that on Rahab, Satan and his princes were able to clone animals with the beings that lived on the planets to reproduce them to modify their genes. He was using Rahab as his space, chemical, or science laboratory.

Heylael used Rahab for experimenting by mixing and genetically altering to manipulate the genes of animals and other creatures. He began to use these beings for merchandising and trafficking. Gene trafficking, drug trafficking, and even humanoid trafficking are examples of what Heylael was doing back on the planet Rahab. He made, sold, and peddled different DNA. This was the start of his *anti (instead of) Christ* ideals and the beginning of his commerce, which was an economic system based upon money. It was a political and economical system that Heylael (cherub/man) wanted to turn into a world-order system by getting those on the planets to worship him as god. He fostered in idolatry and all false religions that are still in practice today.

Nothing Satan does is new. The New World Order System, which is about to manifest, is a duplication of this world-order system that was practiced on planet Rahab. This New World Order System allowed Satan to be in control and to be worshipped as god. There is nothing new under the sun (Eccles. 1:9).

Every living thing was supposed to multiply "after <u>its kind</u>" (*species*) according to the book of Genesis. In Genesis, God told all His creation—mankind, plants, trees, and animals—to all reproduce after its own kind, and they did. Nowhere in the Bible do you read about species mixing or crossbreeding. Naturally, it would have been impossible for species to intermingle.

We humans are supposed to reproduce after our own species, but when some of us can't reproduce, some turn to science for help, like test tubes, surrogate parenting, artificial insemination, and some even use turkey basters. I'm sure you have heard of test tube babies.

That's exactly what Satan was doing in his space laboratory. He was taking DNA from different species and manipulating it to create a species that he could control.

God never intended for man or any of those beings to crossbreed or mix. Trees, plants, animals, Angels, and beings were not meant to have their *DNA* mixed. It is also fascinating that in Genesis 1, the word <u>AND</u> is mentioned many times, but if you turn the word <u>AND</u> around, you get <u>*DNA.*</u> The word *genesis* means "the beginning," but it also means genes (is) or genes (are). Satan used his knowledge of creation and genetics to corrupt what God created, made, and formed. It makes you wonder about the myth of King Kong. Did he really exist?

Evolutionists and scientists believe in the Charles Darwin theory of evolution and the origin of the caveman species. It is the belief that man evolved from apes over time. But that is a lie. We did not evolve from apes because we are descendants of Adam and Eve through Abraham. Abraham lived in this world after the flood of Noah's time. Scientists and others have tried to come up with explanations as to how the earth came into existence. Some have suggested the big bang theory. There is no such thing as the big bang theory.

The big bang theory is only a theory that suggests that galaxies, stars, planets, and people sprang from nothing and for no reason. God had a purpose for everything that He made and created.

In the Beginning God, created heaven and the earth. The beings or Angels that lived at that time toiled and labored and would get tired just like we do. So they went to Heylael (Satan), their leader, and complained. He asked them what they wanted him to do. They suggested that he make creatures that could work for them and be used as slaves for Satan, his princes, or for some of the sons of God. So they chose the most incredible creatures they could by mixing their genes. Satan wanted to combine his hybrid image with God's creation to pervert it.

> *The creature whose name you uttered—it exists! All you have to do, he added is bind upon it the image of the gods. The being was already there, on earth. All that was needed to upgrade it to the required level of ability and intelligence to use tools and follow orders was to bind upon it the image (mark) of the gods, to upgrade the existing ape through genetic manipulation . . . Let the workers carry the toil of the gods. (Genesis Revisited, 160)*

It really wasn't evolution. It was devilution. So this anointed cherub, his workers, and magicians came up with their potions and scientific mixtures in the combinations of DNA genomes to come up with the Neanderthal man and all kinds of unusual beings, even the flesh-eating dinosaurs such as the *Tyrannosaurus Rex.*

There were so many combinations of animals and the people that lived in the world that then was, such as griffins, Cyclopes, mermaids, King Kong, werewolves, satyrs, centaurs, Minotaurs, gargoyles, Pegasus, unicorns, vampires, phoenixes, bird men, horse men, hyena men, and all sorts of hybrid beings. Many of the fantasy creatures you see in cartoons and movies really existed in this world. This cherub/man/seraph created fish, reptilian dinosaurs, and unheard-of creatures that were half-man and half-animal.

Look at Isaiah 34:14. "The wild beasts [dry land] of the desert [wilderness] shall also meet [to come in contact with by violence] with the wild beasts [dry land] of the island [any wild creature], and the satyr [a shaggy he-goat] shall cry [shall call out by name] to his fellow [brother, neighbor]; the screech owl [darkness] also shall rest [be put away] there [confusion], and find for herself [a breathing creature] a place [make to live] of rest [put away]."

Again, in Isaiah 13:21-22, "But wild beasts of the desert shall lie there; and their houses shall be full of doleful creatures (Oh! Expression of grief or surprise), and owls shall dwell there, and satyrs shall dance there. And the wild beasts of the islands shall cry in their desolate houses and dragons in their pleasant palaces and her time is near to come, and her days shall not be prolonged."

These beings are going to return. They already existed on planet Rahab and in that world that Heylael ruled.

A satyr is a shaggy, hairy he-goat that is half-man and half-goat that is mentioned in both scriptures above. Satyrs were associated with Pan, a fertility god, and Dionysus, the god of wine and ecstasy. God wants us to know that they did exist and the multitude of merchandising began.

I believe this cherub/man was selling these hybrids for money and jewels, to be used as slaves and servile work. The corruption and iniquity of this traffic came into play. These creatures were hard to control because of their DNA. The violence and corruption began to manifest. Heylael was an insecure being who wanted to be like God and have creatures made in his image and likeness like God.

Isaiah, the Messianic Prophet, prophesied about kingdoms or empires—past, present, and future—that were enemies of God and His people. Babylon represents all kingdoms of confusion that rebelled against God and worshipped a multitude of idols, did sorcery, used enchanters, and did not honor God as the one and only True God. Isaiah is forewarning the world that all kingdoms or countries that practice abominations and challenge God's authority will be destroyed like Sodom and Gomorrah and Rahab to the point that they will never again be habitable nor exist. They were judged and found guilty of intolerable, abominable wickedness.

According to Mosaic Law, stoning was the primary means of execution for all those who were guilty of divination, genocide, idolatry, murder, blasphemy, adultery, and basically all sorts of sin. God brought a fire out of Satan's midst, which was Rahab, and in the center of his greatest planetary kingdom. The rebel Angels on planet Rahab were judged by giant stones. Rahab exploded into pieces of rocks and left over particles were sent up into the orbits of the celestial and terrestrial worlds.

Asteroids and comets impacted the surface of Mars and rocked the planet. The Martian atmosphere was blasted into outer space, and the genetically manipulated flesh-eating dinosaurs, the very image of the Dragon, were destroyed as well. I believe Michael (who is like God) and his Angels cast the Dragon from the third heaven and cast them out into Earth. The very location of the current asteroid belt is where the planet Rahab was located between

Mars and Jupiter. The asteroids are the remnants of the blown-up planet Rahab.

Satan was destroyed (made to wander) from the stones of fire (planets) where he had reigned over literal (material) kingdoms. There is evidence on Mars of a neighboring planet that exploded.

When God cast him out of heaven, he took away his beauty and covering and exposed him as a cherub/serpent/reptile hybrid. He did not take away his ability to create music, to manipulate, control, or distort light and images or his ability to cover or block and control an entire atmosphere.

The unveiled truth of Scripture is that by his appearance and wisdom, the heavens were beautiful, but with rebellion came corruption and death. That is why darkness (death) was upon the face of the abyss (the deep). The book of Psalms and Isaiah verify this.

> Thou hast broken *(crumbled in pieces)* <u>Rahab</u> in <u>pieces</u>, *as one that is slain; thou hast scattered thine <u>enemies</u> with thy strong arm. (Ps. 89:10)*

> *Awake, awake, put strength, O arm of the Lord; awake, as in the <u>ancient days</u>, in the generations of old. Art thou not it that hath cut (break in pieces) Rahab, and wounded the dragon? (Isa. 51:9)*

He had churches or palaces that he was king over when his kingdom was turned upside down. It affected the universe and all of God's creation. Now he wanders the earth, looking for a body to manifest his deceitful agenda and to portray his image and not God's.

The way planet Earth looks now is the same way that planet Rahab looked back in that world that then was.

On the Earth virtually are the same catastrophes that took place on Rahab. The destruction of Rahab destroyed cities created on Earth before mankind. Jeremiah gives evidence of what happened.

Jeremiah 4:23-27, says, *"I beheld the earth, and, lo, it was without form, and void; and the heavens, and they had no light"*— (This sounds just like Genesis 1:2.)—*"And the earth was without form, and void; and darkness was upon the face of the deep. And the Spirit of God moved upon the face of the waters. I beheld the mountains, and lo, they trembled, and all the hills moved lightly. I beheld, and, lo, there was no man [Adam], and all the birds of the heavens were fled. I beheld, and, lo, the fruitful place was a wilderness and all the cities thereof were broken down at the presence of the Lord, and by his fierce anger. For thus hath the Lord said, the whole land shall be desolate; yet I will not make a full end."*

There were no men (mankind or descendants of Adam), yet there were cities that were destroyed by God's wrath. Who lived in these cities? Never in history since the creation of Adam has man been completely destroyed from the face of the earth. We ourselves are descendents of Adam through Abraham.

The inhabitants of those cities were in fact the angelic host and celestial and terrestrial beings. This may also be an explanation to dinosaurs and animals being frozen immediately while eating. According to Job 38:30,

*The waters are hid as with a stone, and the face of the deep is frozen.*

With the destruction of Rahab, light was withheld and so was heat. During this time, all the waters were not separated, which means basically it was a water world. I believe there is some truth to Atlantis. *Wikipedia* says this about Atlantis, *"And the island of Atalantes [translator's spelling; original: Ἀτλαντίς] which was greater than Africa and Asia, as Plato says in the Timaeus, in one day and night was overwhelmed beneath the sea in consequence of an extraordinary earthquake and inundation and suddenly disappeared, becoming sea, not indeed navigable, but full of gulfs and eddies."*

It seems as though this city of Atlantis was buried under the waters, because according to Genesis, the waters were upon the deep. It is also comprehensible that DNA with genetic manipulation took place according to the book of Job. Job 26:5 states,

*Dead things are formed [twist, coil, genetic manufacturing] from under the waters, and the inhabitants thereof.*

This verse speaks of bringing dead things back to life, but notice they were under the waters.

DNA and genetic manipulation took place on Rahab, which led to DNA and genetic mixing and trafficking by Heylael.

# 4

## _Genetic Mixing_

G enetic mixing, genetic engineering, genetic modifying, genetic manipulation, and genetic mutation are all synonyms that have been used to explain the same procedure as in transhumanization.

According to _Webster's Dictionary_, genetic engineering is "the alteration of genetic material, by cutting up and joining together DNA from one or more species of organism, then inserting the result into another organism." The fact that Heylael _"sealed up the sum"_, enabled him to subtract, add, multiply, and divide DNA using formulas in the same way a Scientist or Chemist would.

The goal of genetic engineering is to remove some traits and add one or more new traits to an organism that is not already found in that organism. We have many fruits and vegetables that have been genetically modified.

Because of population growth, scientist and farmers have worked together to produce genetically modified honey, cotton, rice, soybean, sugarcane, tomatoes, corn, potatoes, flax, papaya, squash, and tobacco.

Half of all farms in the United States of America have produced foods on supermarket shelves that contain some ingredient that has had its DNA tampered with by science. The tampering of some of our fruits have produced hybrid fruits, such as a plumot, which was made from a plum and an apricot. We have a grapple from an apple and grapes. It is believed that hybrid fruits offer more fruit and nutrients, and they grow to enormous sizes. They are also sweeter and can grow in and out of season. Just like scientists today have been practicing genetic modification, so has Heylael in the first Earth age.

All the spiritual beings under the rule of Heylael were like humans in that they had to toil and labor. They were tired. I believe that those celestial beings (Angels) went to Heylael and petitioned him to make a being that would be under their rule and authority and would take on their tasks and burdens.

The spiritual beings would then be gods to them. Instead of taking this request to Our Heavenly Father, he coveted the praise and worship that he would receive from these beings. Then he would be their creator. He also thought about all the money and jewels that he could garnish through trafficking and selling DNA from different species to kings and princes under him on Earth and on other habitable planets.

Remember, he "sealed up the sum." He was skilled in all wisdom and learning, including arithmetic, science, chemistry, physics, biology, etc., are just a few of the subjects that he used to his advantage. They had to find a suitable beast to mix their DNA and genes together that walked uprightly.

According to the Sumerian tablets, there are images of test tube mixing with flasks and serpents entwined or wrapped around a pole in DNA double-helix-coil fashion. Heylael created all sorts of hybrid beings that were mentioned in chapter 3.

Many ancient fossils that scientists continue to find today are millions and millions of years old. How can that be? When this earth is supposedly only six thousand years old? Of course, the fossils prove that the earth is more than six thousand years old.

Heylael also had statues and idols built to honor him as a cherub/man. The Sphinx in Africa is a hybrid being with the body of a lion and the face of a man.

The same figure was built on Mars. Scientists have discovered the remains of a city with pyramids and a Sphinx's face.

According to _Nephilim Stargates_ on page 154, "A role reportedly took place between NASA and Disney, as it seemed the agency didn't like what the film _Mission to Mars_ was insinuating; that a discovery had been made of past alien presence on Mars, that an artificial sphinx-like face and pyramidal shapes near it had been discovered, and a 25 year cover-up had been perpetuated by NASA and the US government in collusion with other world powers."

Heylael, who has been around and lived through all three previous earth ages—the original earth, chaotic earth, and the restored earth—is still around and in existence now in our world, but he won't be around for the new heaven and the new earth. The Sphinx that was found on Mars was made in the likeness of Heylael.

# 5

## *Heylael's Willful Fall*

H eylael was a created being. He was not born umbilical cord to umbilical cord like we were. Satan was not begotten by man or born of woman. We are free moral beings with our own free will. God created him for a specific purpose, and because he was created for a specific purpose, he didn't have the right to rebel against God, but he had the ability to choose to rebel.

Heylael desired to be God and not a servant of God. There's no redemption for Angels. The blood of Christ redeemed us from our sins. Spirits and Angels don't have blood. For our redemption, all we have to do is to receive Jesus as our Lord and Savior and all His redemptive work that He provided for us on Calvary's cross.

The Angels are always in God's presence and had knowledge of the glory of God. Therefore, they had no excuse for rebelling against God and turning away from Him. They were not tempted. God did not provide a plan of redemption for the Angels as He did for mankind.

The primary reason that Heylael fell was because he was determined to exercise his own will after he was ejected from his place in Heaven and the heavenlies. He purposed in his heart to be like God. He was determined to emulate God in everything that he did. Isaiah tells us what happened in Isaiah 14:12-17.

> How art thou fallen [be cast down] from heaven O Lucifer [Heylael], son of the morning [boasting son from the beginning]! How art thou cut down to the ground, which didst weaken the nations [people and animals]!
>
> For thou hast said in thine heart, *I will* ascend into heaven. *I will* exalt my throne [canopy, covering] above the stars [princes] of God; *I will* sit [dwell] also upon the mount of the congregation [meeting place], in the sides of the north [Zion]:
>
> *I will* ascend above the heights of the clouds: *I will* be like [compare, resemble] the most High.
>
> Yet thou shalt be brought down to hell [inmate, Hades] to the sides of the pit.
>
> They that see thee shall narrowly look upon thee, and consider thee, saying Is this the man [frail, mortal] that made the earth to tremble [be afraid], that did shake kingdoms [dominions, realms, estates, houses]:
>
> That made the world [globe] as a wilderness [desert] and destroyed the cities thereof; that opened not the house of his prisoners [bound, captives]?

I believe that Satan had his original throne on Rahab, where he was over cities, nations, and people. He kept them bound as prisoners. In verses 16 and 17, God is describing "the world that then was" and everything that took place in it.

Satan used his will to convince others in the prior world that he was god, just as he convinced Adam and Eve in the Garden of Eden that he was god.

God gives all of us, including the Angels, free will and would prefer that we all choose to serve Him and HIM ALONE. Life is about making the right choices.

Before we go any further, there are some interesting things about the number 5. Five times Satan said *I will* in Isaiah 14 and five times God told him what He is going to do to him in Ezekiel 28.

The fifth chapter of Genesis provides us with information about the genealogy or DNA. Christ was pierced five times to represent His victory over death. There are five books of the law, the Pentateuch. *Satan* is mentioned fifty-five times in the KJV. *Devil* is mentioned fifty-five times in the KJV. On the fifth day, the Lord brought forth creatures to serve. There are five fingers and five toes on each hand and foot to represent service. The word *antichrist* is mentioned five times in the KJV Bible. But the word *Christ* is mentioned 555 times and so is the word *righteousness*. Hallelujah! So the number 5 represents service, the law, victory over death, and God's Kingdom.

Satan had a five-point plan just as the pentagram has five points. A star is a rolling ball of gas, not a pentagram that is often used in the occult and is prevalent in the United States of America. A pentagram when turned upside down is also the shape of a goat's head. This is believed in Freemasonry to be Satan's footprint for the fall of the morning star. It is also the symbol for the Baphomet.

This demonic god of Freemasonry is half-female and half-male and symbolizes transformation and transgenders. Between the eyes of the Baphomet is a five-point pentagram or a star as he is hovering above the ground with a goat's head and wings.

The Bible talks about this in Daniel 8:5 (Notice the number 5 again), "And as I was considering, behold _an he goat_ came from the west on the face of the whole earth, and _touched not the ground: and the goat had a_ _notable horn between his eyes._" The KJV Bible is amazing.

Cherubim surrounded the throne of God and were involved in carrying out God's judgment that took place in Heaven. Seraphim were the Fiery, Holy Heavenly Choir that sung praises to God. Heylael provided the theme music because he was the living orchestra and the choir director, but that wasn't enough for him.

When Satan said "I will sit upon the mount of the congregation in Isaiah," he was already in heaven with God, but he wanted to sit on God's throne and take His place in the divine assembly of judgment on the mercy seat.

God told Moses to build a tabernacle, a portable dwelling place for the divine presence of God from the time of the children of Israel's departure from Egypt to the conquering of the land of Canaan while wandering around in the deserts in Exodus. The tabernacle included a Holy of Holies (Most Holy Place) inner sanctuary where the mercy seat awaited the high priest.

In Exodus 37:6-9, in the Holy of Holies, where the high priest went once a year to make the atonement for his sins and the sins of the children of Israel on the mercy seat, where the blood of the sacrifice for sin was sprinkled, was made out of pure gold and fastened with two cherubim on both sides. The cherubim spread out their wings and covered the mercy seat. The outstretched wings of the cherubim were to provide a throne for God where He would mediate His rule on the earth as a representation of the real throne in heaven. Cherubim were also in the Garden of Eden.

When Adam and Eve sinned by listening to the devil, God sent them out of the Garden of Eden, and cherubim were summoned to guard the way to the tree of life, which was symbolic of Jesus Christ, our Tree of Life.

Cherubim are used to guard and protect Jesus's throne, the mercy seat, and His holiness in Genesis 3:23-24. There is blood on this mercy seat, and DNA is in blood. This mercy seat represented the DNA(life) of Jesus. Jesus said in John 14:6, "I am the way, the truth, and the life: no man cometh unto the Father, but by me."

Heylael was the covering on the top of the mercy seat like a canopy. He covered the throne in heaven. To get to God or His throne, the pre-Adamic creation had to go through Satan to get to God. Satan was the veil that separated God's throne from anyone trying to come to Him uninvited. All uninvited would be consumed by God's holiness and glory. So Satan was protecting, in a sense, the uninvited from being destroyed. In Hebrews 9, Paul talks about the mercy seat in verse 5, "And over it [the mercy seat] the cherubim of glory shadowing the mercy-seat of which we cannot now speak particularly." Because there's more information available about these cherubim now, but the typical meaning of the mercy seat can be found in Romans 3:23-25.

> For all have sinned, and come short of the glory of God; Being justified [just as if we never sinned] freely by His grace through the redemption that is in Christ Jesus; Whom God hath set forth to be a propitiation through faith in His blood, to declare His righteousness [right standing with God] that he might be just, and the justifier of him which believeth in Jesus. [Another name for the mercy seat is propitiatory seat, where Jesus completely removed all our sins once and for all.]

Jesus is our mercy seat because His blood was sprinkled or shed for our sins. God sent Jesus to be our propitiation for our sins (1 John 4:10). When Jesus died on the cross, He rent or tore the veil that separated us from God in Mark 15:38, Hebrews 6:19, and Matthews 27:51. The veil is His flesh (Heb. 10:20). So "Let us therefore come boldly unto the throne of grace that we may obtain mercy, and find grace to help in time of need" (Heb. 4:19). We can come to the throne of grace at anytime in prayer by faith. We are always welcome in our Father's house. We, the Church, the Bride of Christ, took Satan's place in Heaven, and he doesn't like it or us.

Heylael is an imitator, not an initiator. God demoted him from a king to a prince. That is why he is called the prince of the power of the air. We have power and authority over him, as long as we are in line with God's word and use our authority over him in Jesus' Name and put on the armor of God according to Ephesians 6:11-18,

> Put on the whole armour of God that ye may be able to stand against the wiles [tricks] of the devil. For we wrestle not against flesh and blood, but against principalities, against powers, against the rulers of the darkness of this world, against spiritual wickedness in high places. Wherefore take unto you the whole armour of God that ye may be able to withstand in the evil day, and having done all, to stand. Stand therefore, having your loins girt about with truth and having on the breastplate of righteousness: And your feet shod with the preparation of the gospel of peace: Above all, taking the shield of faith, wherewith ye shall be able to quench all the fiery darts of the wicked. And take the helmet of salvation, and the sword of the Spirit, which is the word of God: Praying always with all prayer and supplication in the Spirit, and watching thereunto with all perseverance and supplication for all saints.

Heylael's princes are the fallen angels or celestial beings posing as aliens. They are the same beings who were kicked out along with the dragon from the planet Rahab. Satan is a cherub/seraph/man that can imitate anyone of those beings that he ruled. "The seraph [seraphim], were powerful Angels known for their brilliance, some of which may have followed Lucifer in the fall. Are such fiery flying seraph the source of UFOs today?" (*Nephilim Stargates*, 149). I believe that these seraphs, serpent-looking alien beings were cast out with Satan. For the devil and his angels to manifest, they have to imitate many forms, even man. "And no marvel: for Satan transformed himself into an angel of light. Therefore it is no great thing, if his ministers also be transformed as the ministers of righteousness, whose end shall be according to their works" (2 Cor. 11:14-15).

Even after being booted out of heaven, he and his demons can still trick or deceive, but God has already doomed them to be destroyed, as stated in Matthew 25:41,

> Then shall he say also unto them on the left hand, Depart from me, ye cursed, into everlasting fire, prepared for the *devil and his angels*.

Satan or the dragon had his own angels that he had charge over, which are the aliens of today, and they are significantly different from demons.

They are even mentioned in the book of Hebrews 11:34, "Quenched the violence of fire, escaped the edge of the sword, out of weakness were made strong, waxed valiant in fight, turned to flight the armies of the *aliens*." The word *alien* here means not one's own, foreign, stranger, different, another. And that's what they look like, strange beings from a different or another world. The word *alien* and *aliens* are mentioned eight times in the Bible. Eight represents the number for circumcision or being cut off. On the eighth day, the newborn male was to be circumcised, representing new beginnings. Could that be why these aliens appear to be without genitals or belly buttons?

It is unfortunate that the church and its leaders choose to be ignorant to the fact that the world that then was, existed and the same patterns of behaviors that were rampant then are rampant now. "For this they willingly [choose] are ignorant [to lie hid] of, that by the Word of God the heavens were of old [former, long ago] and the earth standing out of the water and in the water; Whereby the world that then was being overflowed [surge] with water, perished" (2 Pet. 3:9). This verse speaks of an ancient world that was certainly covered by water. During the time of Noah's flood, the waters increased; this was not just a surge. All the flood gates were opened to wash away the sin and rebellion. So that means that Genesis 1:3 through 25 is an account of recreating or restoring Earth.

# 6

## *Recreation of Earth*

God had to destroy the previous _worlds_ that existed by washing them clean with water. "Through faith we understand that the _worlds_ were _framed_ [frames, mend, restore] by the word of God, so that things which are seen were not made of things which do appear" (Heb. 11:3). Did you notice that the word _framed_ means to repair, to mend, and to restore? This is precisely what God did. He restored Earth. He called out those things that did not appear to make them appear by the word of God. It should also be noted that the word _world_ is plural, "_worlds_." It was "by His Son whom He hath appointed heir of all things, by whom also He made the worlds" (Heb. 1:2). This emphasizes the fact that by faith through the word, we are able to call forth things that do not appear and make them appear by faith. Like when we say, "But God shall supply all your [my] need according to His riches in glory by Christ Jesus" (Phil. 4:19). We say that all my needs and bills have already been paid in full according to God's word.

The very first thing God restored was light when He said, "Let there be light." According to John 1:3-4, "All things were made by Him; and without Him was not anything made that was made. In Him was life; and the life was the light of men." So God said let there be life, DNA, power, energy, and truth because life is the light. Darkness represents death, sorrow, misery, Satan, and his kingdom. God called the light day and the darkness he called night. The word *night* means to twist away like a winding spiral staircase.

The DNA double-helix genome looks like a winding spiral staircase. It is as if God was separating His true DNA (life, light) from the corrupt, and the polluted DNA (darkness, night). The Hebrew word for the word *night* is *lel*, which sounds like the ending in *Heylael.* The Spirit of God was brooding over the waters to protect the DNA of the life of God, which is in everything that He made.

In Genesis 1:7-8, it states, "And God made the firmament, and divided the waters which were under the firmament from the waters which were above the firmament: and it was so. And God called the firmament Heaven. And the evening and the morning were the second day." The word *firmament* means expanse, overlay, something spread out. There are three heavens. The first heaven is earth's atmosphere, the sky in the clouds. The second heaven is the outer space where the stars and the planets are located. The third heaven is where God's throne is and where Heaven is located. When God kicked Heylael and his angels out of heaven, they fell first to the second heaven, and that is where he has set up his kingdom. God set up a division between his kingdom and Satan's kingdom. He placed waters above and waters below. The number 2 represents division, separation, and judgment.

The firmament is a boundary between God's heaven and man's heaven. Before now, all the waters were gathered together and collected in one place and location. It is clear that night and darkness represent Satan and the shadow of death. What color are shadows? Shadows are black or dark images that are reflected on anything with the help of the sun. God took away Satan and his fallen angels' beautiful looks and the light of God and cursed them into grotesques beings covered with darkness. In Psalm 44:19, "Though thou hast sore broken us in the place of dragons, and covered us with the shadow of death." There was a place for dragons, and that place is the shadow of death in the second heaven. Another fact that stands out is that all the other days of recreation in Genesis, God said, "and it was good."

He did not call the second day good because He had to separate (put a veil) between Himself and His creation. Heaven used to be one big place until sin and rebellion took place with Satan and a third of the angels. God had to close off heaven with a curtain to separate Himself from the sin.

Even though God separated the third heaven from the second heaven, He made lights in the firmament to act as portals or openings to where the light and the light of God would shine on His creation and reflect His glorious image. One of the definitions for _light_ is "to birth or bring forth and illuminate." The light shines in the darkness, and the darkness cannot overpower it. Satan and his princes cannot stand the true light of God or keep God's creation in darkness (like my dream) and cannot lure us to hell unless we allow it.

The devil hates everything that was created by God, especially mankind, because we were created in His very image and likeness. After everything was restored, God needed someone to take the place of Heylael, who was once God's High Priest, and His prism to reflect His image. He would basically need to create a being to be God in the Earth, a vessel that would reflect the glory of God in the Earth with all the authority and dominion that Satan once had in Heaven.

When we are born of the Spirit and filled with the Holy Spirit, then we can live holy on this earth and truly reflect God's image in everything we say and do, because according to 2 Corinthians 5:17, "Therefore if any man be in Christ, he is a new creature: old things are passed away; behold all things are become new." Our spirit is then recreated like God because He is a Spirit.

# 7

## *In His Image*

Charles Darwin and his theory of evolution and many other scientists would have you believe that we are not made in the image of God and we were not created by God. But I'm going to show you scriptures that tell us that we were created by Him and Him only. When God first created the heavens and the earth in Genesis 1:1, all the Angels or sons of God were present. So that means that they were with Him when He recreated the Earth. In Job 38:4 and 7, *"Where wast thou when I laid the foundations of the earth? Declare, if thou hast understanding. When the morning stars sang together, and all the sons of God shouted for joy?"* The morning stars are the sons of God and a part of God and His Divine Council.

The word *God* in Genesis 1 is used in the plural as in Elohim. There is one God but there are many sons of God who act as one with Him. Look at this verse in Genesis 1:28, "And God (Elohim) said, "Let us make man in Our image and after Our likeness, and let them have dominion over the fish of the sea, the fowl of the air, and over the cattle, and over all of the earth, and over every creeping thing that creepeth upon the Earth." I believe that in the congregation of the other sons of God, they asked Him to let them make man in their image and their likeness, perhaps hybrids like them or equal to them so that man could not rule over them. If we search the scriptures, we see that God does have a Divine Council that acts in unison with Him and the Word (Jesus).

Psalm 82:1, "God standeth in the congregation [company of witnesses who duplicate and repeat] of the mighty: He judgeth among the gods." Furthermore, in Psalm 97:9, "For thou, Lord art high above all the earth: thou art exalted far above all gods." Again, in Psalm 89:7, "God is greatly to be feared in the assembly (secret council, in close deliberation, to consult) of the saints [holy ones, Angel, clean], and to be had in reverence of all them that are about him."

God has His throne, and it is high and elevated; and He has a council of gods (sons of God or the Angels) around Him. A secret council are those who He listens to, who duplicate and repeat His judgments, and who decrees. So when Genesis states, that "God said;" it means that, The Beginning God spoke it first and the Elohim repeated His word the same way that we are supposed to repeat His word. There are Elohim but God Almighty is El. There is scriptural evidence of this Divine Council of God and the sons of God at work when they requested that man be made in their image and likeness. When we are filled with the Holy Spirit, our spirit resembles God and His image.

There was an instance when the King of Judah under Jehoshaphat wanted to know if he and the King of Israel would win a battle that they were about to fight, so they summoned Micaiah (who is like Jah), son of Imlah (full, fill), a true prophet of God, concerning this matter.

The King of Israel gathered four hundred prophets together to ask if he and Jehoshaphat should fight against Ramoth-gilead and win. They told them to go and fight and they would win the battle, but Jehoshaphat wasn't satisfied with what the four hundred prophets had said. He asked if there was another prophet that he could ask. Jehoshaphat asked Micaiah, but the King of Israel said that Micaiah always prophesied bad things against him.

In 1 Kings 22:18-23, "And the king of Israel said unto Jehoshaphat, Did I not tell thee that he would prophesy no good concerning me, but evil? And he [*Micaiah*] said, _Hear_ thou therefore the word of the _Lord sitting on His throne_, and all the host of heaven _standing by Him on His right hand and on His left_. And the Lord said, who shall persuade Ahab, that he may go up and fall at Ramoth-gilead? And one said _on this manner, and another said on that manner_. And there came forth a spirit, and stood before the Lord, and said, I will persuade him. And the Lord said unto him, wherewith? And he said, I will go forth, and I will be a lying spirit in the mouth of all his prophets. And he said, Thou shalt persuade him, and prevail also: go forth, and do so. Now therefore, behold, the Lord hath put [allowed] a lying spirit in the mouth of all these thy prophets, and the Lord hath spoken evil concerning thee."

God allowed the evil spirit to become a lying spirit for evil Ahab. God does have a counsel whom He listens to. He will receive their opinions, suggestions, and involve them in decision making, but ultimately, He makes the final decision. This is an excellent example of God's counsel at work.

Every verse in Genesis 1 begins with the word *and*, except verses 1 and 27. The number 27 represents secrets. In Daniel, the twenty-seventh book of the Bible, He is called, "God, Revealer of secrets." The word *secrets* has something to do with DNA (Psalm 139:13-15). In Genesis 1:26, The Elohim state, "Let _us_ make man in _our_ image and after _our_ likeness." But in Genesis 1:27, "So God created man in _His_ image [representative figure] in the image of God created _he Him_; male and female created _He_ them." What happened to the word *us*? This is why in the very first verse of Genesis, "In the Beginning God," is set apart as the "Word," and Creator. I believe God did this in secret and made us in His very image. Genesis 5:1 reads, "This is the book of the generations of Adam. In the day that God created man, in the likeness of God made _he_ him."

Mankind is made in the image of God, not the image of the sons of God, the Angels. Man did not evolve from apes, nor was man created by the alien beings who are really cherubim/seraphim/ and fallen angels. The reason that this verse does not begin with *and* like the rest of the verses in Genesis 1 is because He wanted it to stand out to get our attention.

Since the recreation of Earth and creation of man, Heylael (Satan) has worked behind the scenes, directly and indirectly conspiring to deceive and destroy the Most High's plans and His image, us humans.

# 8

## <u>Antichrist's Image</u>

The word *antichrist* is defined as "instead of or in place of Christ" or "in place of the anointed one." Satan stated in Isaiah, "I will be like the most high." This statement implies that he covets everything that God has, including and mainly His image on the earth. Here is a fictional account of what Satan is saying to his fallen angels or alien beings, "Come forth flying serpents, you deceive ones with your gray legions, come forth, for the time of my wrath is come. The humans have chosen the forbidden technology, and a body has been prepared for me. I will be born the son of perdition of their choosing. At their invitation I will walk on the earth and enslave the Most High's creation. I will reclaim my former glory, the glory I had when I governed the Galaxy, before the time of the fall. I will revisit the stones of fire [Mars and

Niburu, Rahab, and Planet X], and I will conquer those who wear my mark when I am called the beast," (*Nephlim Stargates*, 115). He wants to replace God with his image. God's seat (throne) must be glorious for Heylael to want to sit on it.

Earlier, I talked about prisms and how Heylael was like a prism that reflected the image of God. Now man is made in that image and is supposed to reflect the image and glory of God. Heylael is the image of the antichrist and refracts away the image of God and reflects the image of darkness and false light. The antichrist will be a hybrid being.

He will be a mixture of different creatures, like what he was doing on planet Rahab. Prisms absorb white light and reflect the seven colors of the rainbow, similar to the 7 Spirits of God, and like the stones that were on Heylael and the high priests of Israel.

There are seven spirits, seven lamps, seven days of the week, and seven notes on a music scale. The number 7 is perfection, completion, and the Word of God. Satan would have us focus on the number 7 in seven dwarfs, seven chakras (the centers of spiritual powers in the human body usually considered to be seven in number by the Hindu religion according to *Wikipedia*), seven heads and ten crowns of the beast, and seven spirits of the antichrist. Satan wants to bring the entire world under the dominion of the antichrist and his system.

He is bringing about a New World Order System to mimic the system that he ruled over in "the world that then was." He (Satan) has worked in seven stages to bring about the antichrist's rule and reign through transforming and altering the image and likeness of mankind.

In Ezekiel 1:28, we find the glory around God and His throne. "As the appearance of the bow that is in the cloud in the day of rain, so was the appearance of the brightness round about. This was

48

the appearance of the likeness of the glory of the Lord. And when I saw it, I fell upon my face, and I heard a voice of one that spake." On top of the throne was a bow. Then in Revelation 4:3, it reads, "And he that sat was to look upon like a jasper and a sardine stone: and there was a rainbow round about the throne, in sight like unto an emerald." An emerald is the color *green,* and green represents life (trees, plants, grass, etc.) It is like living DNA. He is the Living God! Rainbows are seen above the clouds where Satan wanted to elevate his throne. God gave the rainbow as a sign to Noah that He would never again destroy the earth with a flood, in Genesis 9:13.

Again, we see a rainbow in Revelation 4:3 and Revelation 10:1 when talking about God's throne and His clouds of glory that reflected onto everything and anyone in His presence. John mentioned someone (an impostor) riding on a white horse in Revelation 6:2. "And I saw, and behold a white horse: and He that sat on Him had a *bow [simplest fabric, to produce from seed, be born]*; and a crown was given unto Him: and He went forth conquering, and to *conquer [overcome]."*

Satan wants to be and look like the Most High. The rainbow on his head is a cheap imitation. The word *bow* also means "to bring forth seed." That has to do with DNA. The antichrist is a hybrid being who wants to bring forth hybrid beings on earth again. He comes on a white horse, imitating Jesus in Revelation 19. Sometimes the color white can represent death, as when Joseph intepreted the baker's dream of white baskets to mean that he would be hanged. And he was. Satan has always been jealous of God, like Joseph's brothers were jealous of him. Joseph's brothers took away his coat of many colors (like a rainbow). They did not realize what they were doing, like those who worship the Baphomet. I will discuss this later in another book.

Earlier, I talked about Baphomet, a he/she-goat with a rainbow arched over its head that is to represent the prism and Satan's all-seeing eye or third eye. A *prism* is a triangle that transforms light that comes in one way and goes out another. Satan is not all-seeing. God is omnipresent, omniscient, and omnipotent. Satan has and continues to use his network of familiar spirits. A Baphomet is the god of transformation, the god of Freemasonry, and I believe, a transgender because a Baphomet looks like part-man and part-beast (goat equipped with wings) and part-female. It is the exact image of the spirit of the antichrist. There is even a hand gesture with the pinky and the index finger raised and the other fingers pointed downward that shows allegiance to the Baphomet. Satan wants to give man a "beast's heart" like in Daniel 4:16. Satan wants to transform man into goats. God separates the sheep from the goats. It is a belief that the Baphomet is the symbol of homosexuality, transgenderism, and a mixture of opposites with what could be a contamination of DNA. A Baphomet sits in the position with its legs folded like they do in yoga.

Yoga is believed to be the transformation of mind, will, consciousness, and body. This opens one up to demonic possession and control and allows demons to slowly change their DNA.

When I was little, I used to watch a show called *Transformers*. On this show, robots transformed into cars or airplanes, and they could talk. The motto was "More than meets the eye." According to Romans 12:1-2, God tells us, through the writing of Paul, "I beseech you therefore brethren, by the mercies of God, that ye present your bodies a living sacrifice, holy, acceptable unto God, which is your reasonable service. And be not conformed to this world: but be ye transformed by the renewing of your mind, that ye may prove what is that good, and acceptable, and perfect, will of God." The word *conformed* means "to be fashioned like or made in the same pattern and joined to the world and its patterns and circumstances." We are instructed to love not the world or the things that are in it. The Antichrist's philosophy is the exact opposite.

There are many carved statues, images, and pictures of Jesus with long flowing hair down to his shoulders. This is really an image of Zeus, a powerful Greek god of mythology. Zeus is Apollo's father and the Greek word for *perdition*, is *apoleia* (apollo). *Perdition* is mentioned in the Bible in 2 Thessalonians 1:3-4. "Let no man deceive you by any means: for that day shall not come, except there come a falling away first, and that man of sin be revealed, the son of perdition; Who opposeth and exalteth himself above all that is called God, or that is worshipped; so that he as God sitteth in the temple of God shewing himself that he is God."

Also, in John 17:12, "While I was with them in the world, I kept them in thy name: those that thou gavest me I have kept, and none of them is lost, but the son of perdition; that the scripture might be fulfilled." Perdition is ruin, loss, destruction, death, and waste, according to Strong. The son of perdition is Satan. In Revelation 9:11, "And they had a king over them, which is the angel of the bottomless pit, whose name in the Hebrew tongue is Abaddon, but in the Greek tongue hath his name Apollyon, a destroyer."

Many who worshiped Zeus worshiped the earth, statues, idols, altars, and transgender images.

When men dress up like women and women dress up like men, whose image are they portraying? Satan uses the rainbow as the symbol of the new age and androgyny, male and female mixed together and for the LGBT (lesbian, gay, bisexual, transgender).

In the LGBT gay pride movement, they usually march with rainbows and flags showing that they are proud of what they are. Even President Obama, who is a big proponent and an outspoken driving force behind the gay pride movement, was pictured on the cover of *Newsweek* magazine with a rainbow halo over his head with the caption reading, "The First Gay President." Could it be a coincidence that when his stage was erected for his acceptance speech in the 2008 Democratic Convention, he chose to have it constructed as the exact replica of the altar of Zeus, a Pergamon

Altar? In Revelation 2:12-13, "And to the angel of the church in Pergamos write: These things saith he which hath the sharp sword with two edges; I know thy works, and where thou dwellest, even where Satan's seat is: and thou holdest fast my name, and hast not denied my faith, even in those days wherein Antipas was my faithful martyr, who was slain among you, where Satan dwelleth." He is not the Antichrist, but could he (Obama) be an Antichrist? First John says that there are many antichrists in the world.

Homosexuality delineates the very image and likeness of God Almighty. The United States Congress and Senate have begun to push the LGBT agenda onto children. This is a travesty in itself because children are not sexually active, so why introduce this philosophy into their lives? Satan wants to birth and develop his Antichrist image on earth.

In July 2011, the first outwardly open gay United States Senator from San Francisco, Mark Leno, was responsible for initiating and the passing of SB 48, which ensures that the historical contributions of lesbians, gays, bisexual, and transgender people are accurately and fairly portrayed in historical textbooks.

California SB 48 does four main things, but I will highlight the main three:

1. All schools in California must use materials, including textbooks, that include the role and contributions of homosexuals and transgenders to the economic, political, and social development of California and the United States of America with particular emphasis on portraying the role of these groups in contemporary society.
2. No textbooks or instructional materials in California schools may reflect adversely on homosexuality.
3. All alternative or charter schools in California are hereby warned that they'd better adopt similar rules.

Satan has always been after the children, and his methods have not changed. He successfully removed prayer from schools to keep God out. He has managed to promote and encourage abominable sin in schools. It is interesting to note that at the time of the writing of this book, legalization of same-sex marriage is rampant throughout America. Even Governor Jerry Brown recently approved a bill that would allow transgender males and females to use the restroom of their choice. If Satan can continue to block the light of God from entering and manifesting in our lives, he can receive worship from creation as they try to look like Heylael and not God.

Heylael casts a shadow of darkness and death while God casts no shadow. God doesn't have a shadow because in Him there is no darkness, or shadow of turning, only light. That is why iniquity was found in Satan because the image of light that he reflected turned into darkness that represented sin and the curse. Heylael is an imitator and uses his people to imitate him. If you look and act like Satan, then you represent him. Satan is a supernatural hybrid beast that desires for mankind to worship him and his image and look like him. He replaced the image of God with an Antichrist (instead of) image. This is the same mentality and globally dominant system he used in the world that then was.

# 9

## Worshipping the Beast's Image

In the world that then was, all the people and beings were deceived, coerced, bullied, persuaded, and convinced that they should worship Heylael and look like him. He is a beast (dragon), and according to Revelation 20:2, all those that received the mark (identity) or DNA of the beast and worship his image (resemblance, representation) will be cast alive into the lake of fire. Satan had convinced a third of God's children to sin and go into rebellion by worshipping him and idols instead of the Almighty Father God. There are valuable lessons to be learned concerning worship by analyzing the events of rebellion described in Exodus 32, which I will discuss in chapter 10.

Sin has consequences. The more serious the sin, the more serious the consequence. The sins of the Israelites led them to worship idols instead of God. This pattern of idolatry was set in place on planet Rahab by Heylael. God clearly told them as well as us not to worship idols in any form. The worship that we offer to God cannot be perverted when we worship Him in spirit and in truth. The devil operates in the flesh and perversions of the truth. There are some serious matters of judgment that await those who worship the beast (wild, venomous destruction). Many are saying they don't worship the beast. And that they have never gotten down on their knees and praised Satan. There's more to worship than getting down on your knees.

Worship can be defined as "association." According to the *American Heritage College Dictionary*, worship is "the act of reverent love and devotion toward a deity, an idol, or a scared object." Worth-ship is to give worth to something or to make anything valuable for importing, exporting, and for trade. Satan's own slave trade of defiled DNA is the same type of trading that took place in the former world, according to Ezekiel 28. Consequently, Satan was behind the diabolical slave trade of many black people that took place on a ship.

Association is stronger, more powerful, and more important than most people seem to realize. Heylael coveted the worship of God's creation not only because he was insecure and jealous, but he also knew that if he could receive the worship of God's creation, then he could control them along with the surrounding atmosphere and climate and create strongholds over them.

In Genesis 13:18, God told Abraham to go to the plain of Mamre in Hebron where many of the Nephilim (giants) dwelt. The word *Hebron* means "to associate, to join, a society, a spell, or an enchantment." When you worship Satan and his image, you are associating yourself with him and are allowing yourself to be put under his spell, enchantment, or control. God wanted to show

Himself strong in the midst of the people through Abraham so that Satan could not control Abraham like he did the atmosphere.

Satan tried to manipulate and block the light of God from reflecting here on Earth. Satan believes that he is the illuminated, and he illuminates his children with his false light. His followers believe that they are the enlightened ones. They believe that they have the DNA and bloodline of the elite, which is none other than Satan himself.

He is the chief head of the Illuminati. He initiates members and practices witchcraft in the occult to cast spells and enchantments over his followers, which is the same trick that he used in the Garden of Eden. I believe the Illuminati is a group or society of Nephilim, demons, and/or people who believe they are illuminated with knowledge from Lucifer (Heylael) and that a new world order system should be used to control the masses. I believe that from historical information, many secret societies have been formed under the control of the Illuminati, including Freemasonry. Satan uses the Illuminati (his society of people and beings) to magnify his image and agenda through the latest fashions, fads, and trends that are promoted through some music, movies, advertisements, and the media by some celebrities, some athletes, and some famous people. Many people don't really know how or why fads originated before deciding to conform to what they see or hear, like the wearing of sagging pants. They just started wearing sagging pants because they were in style.

The style of wearing sagging pants with underwear exposed originated in the prisons in the United States in the 1960s.

Back then, prisoners were not allowed to have belts because some used them to commit suicide.

Later, homosexual rape became a norm in prisons. When a man wanted another man as a "girlfriend," he would force or rape the man into submission. Afterwards, he would make his "girlfriend" wear his pants below his backside to show that he was "taken" by another man. Whose image or what message are you portraying when you wear sagging pants?

Satan wanders the earth, looking for a person to portray his image as the beast and worship him. We need to be mindful of who we just hang around with. Have you heard the old cliché "association brings assimilation"? The people that you associate with will eventually influence your behavior and lifestyle. Show me your friends, and I'll show you your future. Paul tells us in 2 Corinthians 6:14, "Be ye not unequally yoked together with unbelievers [family members, friends, or associates who don't believe the same as you]: for what fellowship hath righteousness with unrighteousness? And what communion hath light with darkness?" Their bad behavior will rub off on you faster than your good behavior on them.

Worship or association is identified through objects, such as idols, and, more specifically, can include things like how we dress, what we wear, music, jewelry, and markings on our body. All these things are not inherently good or evil, but it is based on what these things are associated with. It is important because it affects our thoughts and choices that we make in life. By wearing the clothing of some famous actors, some athletes, and some recording artists, we can make them modern-day idols. But what do some of the symbols mean?

The image of the skull and the crossbones on clothing represents death. When David killed Goliath, he cut off his head and buried it in a place the Bible calls Golgotha, the place of the skull. This is where we get the word *goth*. It is associated with death and destruction. This is the same place where Jesus was crucified in Matthew 27:33. It is a fulfillment of the prophecy in Genesis 3:15, where the promised seed, Jesus, would bruise the seed of Satan's (Goliath, Nephilim) head.

According to the KJV Companion Bible, "Golgotha was like an elevation of head and shoulders or neck." Remember, Goliath is called the Philistine's champion in 1 Samuel 17:51, and champions are hoisted above and elevated on the team's or people's shoulders. Probably the same way that Heylael had his followers or fans hoist him up, but Jesus flipped it with His birth, death, and resurrection. Jesus is the champion and, because of Him, so are we, according to Romans 8:37. "Nay, in all these things we are more than conquerors through him [Jesus] that loved us."

Even the Batman series takes place in fictional Gotham City, where Batman is clad in black gear just like the school and public mass shooters.

The Columbine shooters wore black and were into goth. More recently, the shooter in Aurora wore all black when he went on his killing rampage and dyed his hair orange to look like the Joker in the Batman movies. The name *Aurora* was on a building in the most recent Batman movie before the senseless killing happened. The shooter in the Sandy Hook killings wore all black. Even more eerie is, the police officer in the Batman movie pointed his finger randomly on a map and it landed on a city named Sandy Hook. All these satanic killers wore black.

The skull and the crossbones is a logo for a fraternity and is a symbol of death. The crossbones are shaped like an *X*, which is supposed to symbolize the X chromosomes. The X chromosomes carry the DNA.

Because the Illuminati controls the media and the contents of it, some celebrities are allowed to promote the whole goth look with black clothes, lipstick, fingernail polish, black eye shadow, black eyeliner, etc. Can you believe that there is even Christian goth? The same way Heylael desired and demanded the adoration of his followers, the Illuminati's celebrity puppets demand the same. It's as if they put people under a spell. Like in my dream, everyone was in black. Black is the absence of light, not darkness. God called the light day, and the darkness He called night. Satan operates in darkness.

Satan is the master musician. He uses the lyrics, beats, and the atmosphere that music can create, to his advantage. He uses some music celebrity icons like rappers, singers, producers, songwriters, and people who play instruments to influence people to worship his image or the reflection of the beast unknowingly. Some tattoos, body piercing (tongue, genitals, eyebrows, lips, nose, or basically anywhere on the body), and body art have become modern-day symbols of worship towards Satan and the culture that he created in the world that then was and in the world that we live in now. The tattoos, body piercing, art, and brandings were all ways that the Egyptians worshipped their gods (deities and demons) in Egypt. Every piercing represented praise to that particular god, depending upon their type and ranking. Pharaohs made the Israelites wear these ornaments to give praise to the hundreds of gods that they worshipped. This is another reason why the Sabbath, which is Saturday, is so important because the Israelites were not allowed to keep the Sabbath holy while enslaved. They were made to worship exclusively the Sun god on Sunday.

Even the fad of boys and men wearing two earrings represented bisexuality, and now it is the new style or a fad to do. Alexander the Great, Caesar, Napoleon, and most of the Greek gods wore two earrings because they were bisexual. God told the children of Israel to remove any remnants of the pagan culture from Egypt from their body in Exodus 33:5, "For the Lord had said unto Moses, say unto the children of Israel, Ye are a stiffnecked people: I will come up into the midst of thee in a moment, and consume thee: therefore now put off thy ornaments from thee, that I know what to do unto thee." It was what the jewelry represented and its previous association with idol worship. It is the power of association. The ornaments and jewelry were melted down and used as articles for the tabernacle.

Tattoos and brandings that are used to represent fraternities and sororities are clearly forbidden by God in Leviticus 19:28. "Ye shall not make any cuttings in your flesh for the dead nor print any marks upon you: I am the Lord!" I love the way He ends it with "I am the Lord!" The lord that you are giving worship to through your tattoos is not the true Lord nor should he be your master. God put this in the Bible because he knows it will open you up to demons and demonic control. In various countries like Egypt (Africa), India, China, and Korea, many people identified their relationship and joined their DNA with a particular god by the way they marked their bodies. Tattoos and brandings are marks on people's bodies that can be used to identify a person and their allegiance to someone or something. Cattle and livestock are branded, so why is that a requirement for some fraternities? God would never demand or tell you to get branded or swear an oath to false gods and goddesses as an allegiance or association with a secret society or an organization.

Children are so impressionable. They put their trust in what they see and hear regularly. When they see celebrities, rappers, and other icons with tattoos and brandings, they want to emulate them. It is as if the person wearing the tattoo calls out to whomever or whatever spirits that are implicated by that mark. When this occurs, a door is opened for demons to stay connected to people and follow them around until they are forced to leave. Many people get tattoos for loved ones who have passed on, but God forbids this because it can summon familiar spirits. It is difficult to believe that a person can wear identifying clothing and marks or body art that have associated them with Satan and believe that they can give their whole heart and mind to God. He tolerates "no other gods!" according to Exodus 20:3. Could the ink for the tattoos become embedded in your skin and into your bloodstream and affect your DNA? Does anyone really know what tattoo ink is made from and made of? Some believe that the ink has arson, which is a poison. You can repent from getting tattoos and make sure that you don't get any more. He will forgive you if you are sincere. God could even erase them from your body. Nothing is impossible with Him!

Another area where demons have influence and receive worship is from images in many of our cultures. Many statues, idols, figurines, relics, and pictures have been collected, purchased, and kept in people's houses, offices, cars, and on their bodies. People love to collect items that are either from or represent Africa, Egypt, India, China, and other countries as souvenirs. A lot of African Americans believe that because our ancestors came from Africa, then we have to wear clothing from Africa and collect their artifacts. Africa is not evil in itself, but it is the witchcraft, voodoo, and black magic that has been prevalent there since Adam's fall. Satan brought idolatry from Rahab to Egypt (Africa). Many of these items are idols that were once dedicated to gods, for example, the ankh. The ankh is not a cross, but it represents 360 degrees that God is man and woman. It represents mythical eternal life, rebirth, and the life-giving power of the sun. It symbolizes Osiris, Isis, and Ra, the Egyptian copy of the Holy Trinity. All the Egyptian gods are depicted with an ankh in their hands. Wearing an ankh is in direct objection and violation of the cross (tree) that Jesus was crucified on for our sins.

Many people have African statues, such as Zulu statues and masks. They don't realize that Zulu is a false god in Africa. On the Soul Train Music Awards, the winner would receive a Zulu mask as a trophy. The same is true with Guatemalan, Hindu, Korean, and Chinese statues and voodoo masks and some of their jewelry, ornaments, clothing, and pictures. There are Christians who have statues of Buddha and rub his belly for good luck. If you have any of these items, you need to get rid of them *now*!

Most idols are carved and/or painted to look just like the gods that they represent. Owning these items that were made and designed to give worship to false gods, work like magnets that invite Satan and his demonic host into your life. Another celebration that people need to understand is Mardi Gras.

Mardi Gras is another celebration that a Christian needs to question as to what are the underlying spirits behind the elaborate masks and colorful beads? Mardi Gras, an annual celebration commonly held in New Orleans, Louisiana, where people attend costume balls and catch beads, doubloons, cups, and trinkets that are thrown from floats. Mardi Gras has been used as a time for one of the biggest orgies or parties of drunkenness, lewdness, public nudity, homosexuality, illicit sex, revelry, and brawling, which are all described as works of the flesh in Galatians 5:19-21. Mardi Gras is similar to modern celebrations in Rome where they give themselves to Bacchus, the god of wine, and Venus, goddess of love. Romans wear masks, dress in costumes, and indulge all their fleshly desires as they give themselves to their gods. Roman tribes celebrated a time of renewal of life, which they called Lupercalia, in honor of Lupercus, the Roman god of fertility.

According to *Wikipedia*, Lupercalia, was a drunken orgy of merrymaking held each February in Rome, after which the participants fasted for forty days during Lent. What religion observes Lent? Sounds like Mardi Gras to me. The Greeks did the same thing.

According to Dr. Henry Malone in *Portals to Cleansing* on page 90, in Greece, their god Dionysus was the inventor of revelry. Those who followed Dionysus believed in "letting themselves go and giving themselves over to natural, earthly desires. Wine helped them to achieve a state of enthousiasmos or being outside their body and inside their god." When you celebrate Mardi Gras, which gods are you honoring? What spirits have you invited as a permanent guest that you will have to evict, bind up, and cast out of your heart and house? Dr. Malone says, "You cannot deal with the objects of idolatry in your home until you deal with other gods in your heart."

The Lord did not want the children of Israel to allow any idols into their heart or home, so He told Joshua to destroy Achan and his family and their belongings, in Joshua 8. Joshua burned with fire all the relics that Achan had taken from Babylon along with his family and their belongings because of what they represented. Achan sinned and caused an abomination to come upon the Israelites because of his disobedience and ignorance. Israel lost the battle, and many people lost their lives because of Achan. Unfortunately, ignorance does not protect you from the effects of owning these images. Having these items can and will undoubtedly bring generational curses to you, your family, and the household. Some of these curses include diseases. Demons bring diseases. The New Testament documents more than a quarter of the healings that took place were actually deliverances from demons.

In Deuteronomy 7:25-26, it states, "The graven images of their gods shall ye burn with fire thou shalt not desire the silver or gold that is on them, nor take it unto thee, lest thou be snared therein: for it is an abomination to the Lord thy God. Neither shall thou bring an abomination into thine house, lest thou be a curse thing like it: but thou shalt utterly detest it, and thou shalt utterly abhor it, for it is a cursed thing." Opened doors invite intruders that come to kill, steal, and destroy. *In "Portals To Cleansing," on page 25 Henry Malone states, "We've all bought things, received gifts, inherited items, or purchased souvenirs that have the potential of providing demons a point of entry into our households. Even jewelry, purses, amulets, pictures, clothing, family heirlooms, antiques, and auctioned items may have familiar spirits from dead relatives, past owners, or objects that represent other gods, religion, the occult, or secret societies that must be destroyed. Any object in your home that has a carved, painted, or stone image of an idol, god, or demonic figure should be removed."* Our homes should not have Buddha, fertility gods and goddesses, and Native American, Aztecan, African, Mayan, and Haitian cultural items that are considered to be idolatrous. Ask God about these items by praying over them. He'll let you know what you need to get rid of *immediately!*

We talked earlier about the Baphomet or the transgender androgynous god that is both male and female that is a half-goat and half-human beast that is blurring the lines between men and women, homosexuality, heterosexuality, the secret and profane, and church and the world. It is amazing that some churches have embraced the world, hip-hop, and the music and culture of the world and have not separated themselves from it and the demons that accompany it.

The Illuminati have celebrity men wearing jeggings, makeup, nail polish, and lipstick to deny their biological gender and to blaspheme the image that God created them to be. God doesn't support homosexuality in any form or fashion, in Leviticus 18:22. "Thou shalt not lie with mankind, as with womankind: it is an abomination."

The LGBT would have you believe that Jesus did not deal with the issue of homosexuality, but I beg to differ. In Matthew 9:35, "And Jesus went about all the cities and villages, teaching in their synagogues, and preaching the gospel of the kingdom, and healing every sickness and every disease among the people." The word *disease* here is the Greek word *malakia* or *malakos*, which means softness, debility, effeminate, and catamite. According to the dictionary, a catamite is a boy or man who has a sexual relationship with a man. As you can see, Jesus healed them of this. He did it then, and He can and will do it now. It is interesting how the word *disease* and *homosexuality* are equated in the Bible. God created man for a woman, which is the natural way to reproduce. This is the way God intended and planned from the very beginning, but transgender, homosexual Heylael turned into Satan, our adversary, and his hoards of demons have created the same LGBT world atmosphere here on Earth that he did in the world that then was. We have a choice in this world. We can either be made into the beast's image by following Satan and by worshipping idols or cursed items or be the image of Christ by reading, studying, practicing, repeating by saying, and living the Word of God.

# 10

## DNA

T hroughout this book, you have been reading about DNA, but what exactly is DNA? DNA, Deoxyribonucleic Acid, is made out of nucleotides and deoxyribose, which control our cells. Cells are the building blocks of life. All of us are made out of trillions of cells. Each cell has its own special job to do. DNA functions as the boss that tells each special molecule in each cell what to do. DNA looks like a beautiful curved ladder or spiral staircase that is shaped like a double helix. The rungs on the DNA ladder are special sugars and other atoms that make up the handrails. Notice that in the middle of the word deoxy_rib_onucleic is the word _rib, which_ is not a literal rib.

In Genesis 2:18-25, "And the Lord God said, it is not good that the man should be alone: I will make him an help meet for him. And out of the ground the Lord God formed every beast of the field, and every fowl of the air: and brought them unto Adam to see what he would call them: and whatsoever Adam called every living creature, that was the name thereof. And Adam gave names to all cattle, and to the fowl of the air, and to every beast of the field; but for Adam there was not found an help meet for him. And the Lord God caused a deep sleep to fall upon Adam, and he slept; and He took one of his _ribs_, and closed up the flesh instead thereof; And the _rib(curve)_, which the Lord God had taken from man, made He a woman (womb-man), and brought her unto the man. And Adam said, This is now bone of my bones, and flesh of my flesh: she shall be called Woman, because she was taken out of man. Therefore shall a man leave his father and his mother, and shall cleave unto his wife: and they shall be one flesh. And they were both naked, the man and his wife, and were not ashamed."

In verse 21, the word _ribs_ is in the plural. Why? The reason why the word _ribs_ is used in the plural sense is because all humans possess this two-strand helix in our genetic marking. The curved or twisted helix in our DNA is made up of X and Y chromosomes, which are the two sex chromosomes that determine the gender of a fetus. All females have two X chromosomes and all males have one X chromosome and one Y chromosome.

In the beginning, when God created Adam in Genesis 1:27, "So God created man in His own image, in the image of God created he him; _male_ and _female_ created He them." For what purpose did God create them? God gives us the answer in Genesis 1:28. "And God blessed them, and God said unto them, Be fruitful, and multiply, and replenish the earth, and subdue it: and have dominion over the fish of the sea, and over the fowl of the air, and over every living thing that moveth upon the earth." Inside Adam, God had already placed the DNA to make both of them from the beginning. Eve was not an afterthought. God had her in mind when He created Adam and placed the chromosomes for both male and female inside Adam's body. He just extracted the female chromosomes from Adam to build Eve. God copied His own work genetically when He built Eve and gave her a womb to carry the offspring.

In verse 22 of Genesis 2, we find the word *rib*, which is singular because God had already taken the XX chromosomes from Adam to make Eve (woman) and brought her to Adam. God replicated the DNA of his X chromosomes that were in Adam.

Genetic copying is how replication of the original model, Adam, was done to make Eve. To replicate means to duplicate or a reproduction or copy of a work, especially a copy by the maker of His original. Eve was truly biologically a bone of Adam's bone and flesh of his flesh, and the two of them were one flesh.

Whenever the words "the two became one flesh," God is talking about marriage. God ordained, established, and instituted the sanctity of marriage in Genesis 2:24 between a man and a woman or a male and a female. God said that Eve was Adam's wife. God married or joined them together as husband and wife. To have a marriage in God's eyes, it takes a man and a woman. To be a husband, you must first be a man, and in order to be a wife, you must first be a woman. Everywhere in the Bible where the two are one flesh, God is talking about marriage and sex within the marriage.

In Matthew 19:4-6, Jesus repeated the same words that God told Adam and Eve in Genesis. He said, "Have ye not read, that He which made them at the beginning made them male and female, And said, For this cause shall a man leave father and mother, and shall cleave to his wife: and they twain shall be one flesh? Wherefore they are no more twain, but one flesh. What therefore God hath joined together, let not man put asunder." As far as God is concerned, we're only to have children after we get married.

God established His standards for marriage and who should be the participants in a marriage before there was a court or government to change His rules and regulations for marriage. (See also Ephesians 5:31 and 1 Corinthians 7:2 for more information about marriage.) God chose by making Eve for Adam.

According to Jewish manners, it was the custom of the father to choose whom his offspring would marry. It was customary to marry those within your own bloodline before the laws in Leviticus were written, which normally meant a near relative. Since God was the Father and the Creator of both Adam and Eve, He made the choice to unite them in marriage, and He gave them the Garden of Eden, the Earth, as their home for complete peace, harmony, and happiness.

As Adam and Eve became fruitful, multiplied, and replenished the Earth, sons and daughters were born to them. Just like they were married to each other, when we receive Jesus, the Lamb of God, as our Lord and Savior, we become a member of His church or family, which is the Bride of Christ. As the body of Christ, we take Jesus' DNA and become one with Him. Our DNA is exchanged with His DNA to become one in spirit.

This happened when Jesus died on the cross. In John 19:34, it states, "But one of the soldiers with a spear pierced [prick, nudge] His side, and forthwith came there out blood and water." The word *side* here is the Greek word *pleura*, which means rib (DNA). The same thing occurred with the first Adam, when God took DNA from him to build Eve. There was probably blood and water then too. A person's DNA is used to identify him/her through his/her blood, urine, semen, hair, fingerprints, and/or saliva. The blood and water that came out of Jesus represented His DNA. Because of His blood, we can be born again and receive His DNA that takes away all curses, including generational curses. When a woman gives birth, her water breaks and the baby is born through bloodshed. The blood of Jesus, the Lamb, makes us His bride, and we are to cleave together with His DNA to become one with Him like Adam and Eve.

Adam and Eve's family had grown immensely. They were not only parents but also grandparents and great-grandparents. A particular class of Angels called Watchers are mentioned in Daniel 4:13, 17, and 23 and were watching Adam and Eve and what was happening upon the Earth. Watchers are a special class of Angels that appear to look like men and have interest in the "daughters of men." These Watchers were members of the Divine Council in Heaven. They are the sons of God who married human women and had children by them, according to Genesis 6:1-4. "And it came to pass, when men began to multiply on the face of the earth, and daughters were born unto them. That the sons of God saw the daughters of men that they were fair; and they took them wives of all which they chose. And the Lord said, My spirit shall not always strive with man, for that he also is flesh; yet his days shall be an hundred and twenty years. There were giants in the earth in those days; and also after that, when the sons of God, came in unto the daughters of men, and they bare children to them, the same became mighty men which were of old, men of renown." When they married women, they mixed their angelic DNA with human DNA. Their offspring were called giants or Nephilim.

These Nephilim were hybrid creatures and gigantic mixtures. They were huge. Some of these giants were fifteen, twenty, thirty, and even up to three hundred feet tall and were destroying everything and everyone that God had created. The *Book of Enoch* talks about these sons of God and what they did.

Enoch was Noah's great-grandfather and is mentioned in Jude 14, Hebrews 11:5-6, and Luke 3:57 in the genealogy of Mary, the mother of Jesus. Enoch walked in faith and righteousness the 365 years of his life. God loved Enoch so much that He spared him the experience of death. Enoch was of the generation of Adam and lived when the sons of God lived on the Earth and produced giants.

Enoch talks about these sons of God in his book and what they did. Once these beings willfully left their estates in heaven, they were immediately considered to be fallen. The Watchers, or fallen Angels, are posing as aliens today, but alien or not, they still have to bow or succumb to the name of *Jesus of Nazareth*. It is important to note that after a random survey was taken of alien abductees almost half (500) were Christians. According to their testimony when they used the name of Jesus, the abduction stopped. The book of Revelation calls these Nephilim aliens, "unclean spirits that looks like frogs."

The Hebrew root word for *Nephilim* means "to fall, fall to the ground, fall in battle, or be cast down." These are the fallen ones or the descended ones. If you are wondering how spiritual beings could have intercourse and mix their genes and DNA with human women, the daughters of men, the following excerpt from *Exo-Vaticana* on page 137 explains it. "Ultraterrestrial beings [call them angels, demons, or aliens] can migrate back and forth between different realities and take forms that are both material and immaterial." This sounds crazy to the natural mind, yet the concept is biblical. The writer of Hebrews reminds us to "be not forgetful to entertain strangers; for thereby some have entertained angels unawares" (Heb. 13:2). And when the disciples of Jesus saw His return from the grave, they "were terrified and affrighted, and suppose that they had seen a spirit." Jesus told them to touch Him and see that "a spirit hath not flesh and bones, as ye see me have" (Luke 24:37-39). Similarly, Abraham was visited by three Angels in the plain of Mamre in Genesis 18:1-8. They appeared as men and walked, talked, sat, and ate. But the truth was, they were not human at all but Spirit beings from heaven, illustrating one of the most dynamic facts of Scripture that "other dimensional life forms have power to assume tangible matter whenever it fits their cause" (*Exo-Vaticana*, 137).

When the Nephilim corrupted mankind, God (Yahweh) wiped them out with a flood of gigantic proportions. The Nephilim were neither fully human nor fully angelic, so their spirits had nowhere to go. These spirits became demons or devils, and now they go around looking for bodies and DNA to infiltrate. According to *The Book of Enoch*, "And now the giants who have proceeded from spirits and flesh shall be evil spirits on earth and it shall be their dwelling. Evil spirits have proceeded from their bodies. They shall be evil spirits on earth and the spirits of giants afflict, oppress, destroy, attack, and work destruction on the earth and cause trouble, and shall rise up against the children of men."

According to *Baker's Evangelical Dictionary of Biblical Theology* by Walter A. Elwell, "While the New Testament uses the Greek word, "demon" to refer to these "sons of the mighty," the Old Testament uses revealing descriptive names. Words which describe these beings, such as b'nai Elohim meaning "sons of God," Zophim meaning, "the watchers," and Malakh meaning "messengers," [this reference was translated *angel* in English], are used for the "aerial host" often regardless of alignments." The *Book of Enoch* tells us the origin of certain "interdimensional intelligences" called in the monotheistic New Testament *demons*, who were understandably associated with evil because, originally, the Greek term *diamon* meant "any deity," as it was in the Days of Noah, and didn't end with the Flood but continued, according to Genesis 6, even after. According to Walter Elwell, an evangelical writer agrees with the writers of the books of Luke, Jude, and Paul that Enoch is a reliable source to quote when talking about the giants, Nephilim, and demons.

Demons want to change our DNA to cause diseases, sicknesses, and generational curses. If you search the New Testament, you will notice a link between sickness, disease, and genetic deficiencies and disorders because of demons. Demonic possession can affect DNA and chromosomes. Nephilim (gegenes) is the same word for "Titans" in Greek mythology. The Titans were giants. The words "genes" and "genetics" come from the same word meaning, "genea," breed or kind.

There are Nephilim on Earth today, but they are disguised as humans; and they are not ten, twenty, or thirty feet tall. They look like you and me. Those giants were flesh and blood, but they were humongous. The Nephilim are the tares that Jesus is talking about in Matthew 13:24-30. "Another parable put He forth unto them, saying, the kingdom of heaven is likened unto a man which sowed good seed in his field: But while men slept, his enemy came and sowed tares among the wheat, and went his way. But when the blade was sprung up, and brought forth fruit, then appeared the tares also. So the servants of the house-holder came and said unto him, Sir, didst not thou sow good seed in thy field? From whence then hath it tares? He said unto them. An enemy hath done this. The servants said unto Him. Wilt thou then that we go and gather them up? But He said, Nay: lest while ye gather up the tares, ye root up also the wheat with them. Let both grow together until the harvest. I will say to the reapers, Gather ye together first the tares, and bind them in bundles to burn them: but gather the wheat into my barn." This parable is written in red, so we know that Jesus is the one doing the talking. After Jesus sent the multitude of people away, His disciples wanted to know what the parable about the tares and the wheat meant. Jesus is explaining the parable (secret) in Matthew 13:37-43. "He answered and said unto them, He that soweth the good seed is the Son of Man. The field is the world: the good seed are the children of the kingdom; but the tares are the children of the wicked one. The enemy that sowed them is the devil: the harvest is the end of the world; and the reapers are the angels. As therefore the tares are gathered and burned in the fire; so shall it be in the end of this world. The Son of Man shall send forth His angels, and they shall gather out of His kingdom all things that offend, and them which do iniquity: And shall cast them into a furnace of fire: there shall be wailing and gnashing of teeth. Then shall the righteous shine forth as the sun in the kingdom of their Father. Who hath ears to hear, let him hear."

Jesus is letting us know that Satan has his children or his seed living in this earth with us, God's children. Jesus revealed to His disciple John how to recognize Satan (the beast), his children, the Nephilim, and demons by their mark in Revelation 13:16-18. "And he causeth all both small and great, rich and poor, free and bond, to receive a mark in their right hand, or in their foreheads. And that no man might buy or sell, save he that had the mark, or the name of the beast, or the number of his name. Here is wisdom. Let him that hath understanding count the number of the beast: for it is the number of a man and his number is six hundred threescore and six," which is 666. Let's use wisdom and understanding and count. When you count these things from the above verse; small, great, rich, poor, free, and bond, that equals 6. The mark, name, and number of the beast is his DNA. It is Satan's signature. DNA can read combinations of sequences, letters, and codes like a book. 666 in Hebrew alludes to drug or poison. Could it be that Satan will offer us a DNA upgrade to prolong our life and or to avoid diseases? But it would poison our genetic system and change our DNA? Could this be what happened with Nimrod? According to page 32, in Exo-Vaticana, Tom Horn seems to think so as he translates Genesis 10:8,9. *"And Nimrod began to change genetically, becoming a gibborim, the offspring of the watchers on earth . . . . it rewrote his genetic makeup fashioning him into a fit extension for an otherworldy spirit."*

The number 6 is the number of the image of man and of beast because both of them were created on the sixth day in Genesis 1. Genesis 6 talks about giants (Nephilim). The bible also states that Goliath had 6 fingers and 6 toes. The number 6 also represents preparation, because in Genesis 6 preparations were made for the flood, when Noah built the Ark. "The Days of Noah," is mentioned 6 times. The term "Day of preparation," is used 6 times in the KJV bible. In Exodus 16:5 the Lord told His children to *prepare* the manna on the sixth day. We are in the 6th hour and this book is written to prepare you for what is to come. The third 6 in Revelation 13:18 represents the image of the nephilim, which would make a third strand of DNA, making it a triple helix instead of a double helix. Man's, beast's, and angel's DNA equals 666. That makes a third strand of DNA added to the double-stranded DNA. This illegally turns the double helix of human DNA into a triple helix DNA. The mark in the forehead that is where our brain is located must have something to do with our beliefs, thinking, and with changing our DNA to that of a hybrid, Nephilim, and/or a beast to make us resemble Satan and his fallen angels. In the bible the word Mark is synonymous with the word image. It is true that the Hebrew alphabet is modeled after DNA. The Hebrew word for *letter* is related to the words, *seed,* and *semen.* Remember DNA has genes (letters, sentences) which pass through the seed. Could the mark of the beast vs the mark of Yahweh reflect whose image you are in? The Greek word for mark is *charagma* or *charakter,* which sounds like the word *character.* DNA is the language of the books in our bodies. The sentences are the "genes." There are 22 Amino acids in DNA and 22 letters in the Hebrew alphabet. Amino acids act as proteins. When you break down the word DNA it means *de* (according to, from), *oxi* (sharp, Heb. 4:12), *ribo* (sweet, Psalms 119:103), *nucleic* (seed, Luke 8:11), *Acid* (Olive tree of Life, oil, Romans 11). We will either receive the mark (DNA) of the beast or the seal (DNA) of the Holy Spirit, which is resurrection DNA.

In order for this to occur, we have to be like the King/Priest Melchizedek, who is King of Righteousness and Peace. He is literally "The Word." When He became "The Son" (Jesus), He was made flesh or given human DNA. The same DNA that was protected, prepared, and preserved in the mercy seat in Heaven until His birth on Earth. But according to Psalm 110:4, Jesus is called a Priest forever *after the order of Melchizedek.* This should tell you the greatness of this *man* since Jesus is called after His order (a word, reason, suit, or style or to subdue, arrange, or speak).

The only time we are told about Melchizedek is when He appeared on Earth as King and Priest in Genesis, where everything directly or indirectly has to do with genes or DNA. In Genesis 14, Melchizedek came to Abram before his name was changed to Abraham, Father of many, after he fought and defeated the demonic Nephilim giant kings who kidnapped Lot and his family. He gave Abram bread and wine, Communion, which represented the body and the blood of Jesus and His DNA. In Hebrews 7:1-8 it states, "For this Melchizedec, king of Salem, Priest of the Most High God, who met Abraham returning from the slaughter of the kings, and blessed him; To whom also Abraham gave a tenth part of all; first being by interpretation King of Righteousness, and after that also King of Salem, which is King of Peace: Without father, without mother, without descent, having neither beginning of days, nor end of life; but made like unto the Son of God; abideth a priest continually. Now consider how great this man was, unto whom even the patriach Abraham gave the tenth of the spoils. And verily they that are of the sons of Levi, who receive the office of the priesthood, have a commandment to take tithes of the people according to the law, that is, of their brethren, though they come out of the loins of Abraham; But he whose descent is not counted from them received tithes of Abraham, and blessed him that had the promises. And without all contradiction the less is blessed of the better. And here men that die receive tithes; but there he receiveth them, of whom it is witnessed that he liveth." This means that Melchizedek's genealogy can't be traced. The word *descent* means *genealogetos*, which means "a canceling out of our natural genealogy to make us like the Son of God," Christlike members of the Royal Priesthood that is spoken of in 1 Peter 2:9. "But ye are a chosen (favorite) generation (race), a royal (kingly in nature) priesthood (high priest order), a holy (pure) nation, a peculiar (to show around self as an acquired possession) people; that ye should shew (display) forth the praises (excellence, character) of Him who hath called you out of darkness (shade) into His marvelous light."

Melchizedek originated from a realm that cancels out earthly DNA to make us like Jesus Christ. This is our inheritance as joint heirs with Jesus, the man and our Messiah. We are children of God and heirs of God and partakers and participants with everything that Jesus has done for us according to Romans 8:16 and 17. "The Spirit itself beareth witness with our spirit, that we are the children of God; And if children, then heirs, heirs of God, and joint-heirs with Christ; if so that we suffer with Him, that we may be also glorified together." Our life is hidden with Christ. In order to find or save our life, we must lose it. That is exactly the order of Melchizedek.

DNA produces light. Scientists have discovered that DNA contains biophotons and weak proton emissions (a.k.a light). Based upon John 1:4, "In Him [God] was life; and the life was the light of men." That life is His DNA (power, energy) and light. He is the Father of lights. So that means that His children are to be what? Lights in the Earth.

Paul tells us in Ephesians 5:8, "For ye were sometimes in darkness, but now are ye light in the Lord: walk as children of light."

"Ye are the light of the world. A city that is set on an hill cannot be hid. Neither do men light a candle, and put it under a bushel, but on a candlestick: and it giveth light unto all that are in the house. Let your light so shine before men, that they may see your good works, and glorify your Father, which is in heaven" (Matt. 5:14-16).

Moses's face was shining with the light from God's Shekinah glory when he came down from Mount Sinai. God told Moses to come up a second time to Mt. Sinai because Moses broke all Ten Commandments when he became furious when he witnessed the idolatry of the Israelites. God had to give Moses the Ten Commandments a second time. Moses spent forty days and forty nights with God upon the mount. When Moses came down from Mount Sinai, God's glory was reflected on his face, the same way that Heylael's jewels reflected God's glory. The people were afraid to go near him. After that, Moses had to cover his face with a veil in Exodus 34:30-35. God's light or His DNA is supposed to radiate from us for others to see, like in Stephen.

Stephen was a Christian born and filled with the Holy Spirit or the DNA of God. He was a man full of wisdom and had good standing in his community. The disciples needed to choose one out of seven men to serve tables and wait on the widows of the Grecians and the Hebrews. Stephen was chosen. He did great wonders and miracles among the people. Some of the people told lies about Stephen. He was brought to the council and stoned to death. All people that watched the stoning "saw his face as it had been the face of an angel" (Acts 6:15). There was a bright, shining light coming from his face. It even happened with Jesus on the Mount of Transfiguration. The Bible says in Matthew 17:1-2, "And after six days (there's that number 6 again) Jesus taketh Peter, James, and John his brother, and bringeth them up into an high mountain apart. And was transfigured (changed) before them: and His face did shine as the sun, and His raiment was white as the light." We are light in Christ. We are the image and glory of God in 1 Corinthians 11:7, and we should reflect His image and not our own, like Satan. We have taken Heylael's (Satan's) place.

God's light or DNA has been around since before He created all three world ages. In the Old Testament, His DNA was on His chosen people, but in the New Testament, His DNA is in His children. When we receive Jesus as our Lord and Savior, we receive His DNA. As His children, we are called out of darkness or the living according to the ways of this world. We are a new creation in Christ. The new image of the new man is in Christ, and the only way to be transformed into this new Christlike man or woman is by the Holy Spirit. He can change us and our DNA. Look at 1 Samuel 10:6, which states, "And the Spirit of the Lord will come upon thee, and thou shalt prophesy with them, and be turned into another man." As we partake of the body and the blood of the Lord when we take Communion, we are literally reminding ourselves that Jesus took our old sinful DNA and exchanged it for His eternal, spotless DNA. It is amazing the way Jesus Christ and His body, we the Church or The Bride of Christ, is a special possession that is over and above all else; is a purchased acquisition of high value that is shut up, preserved, and saved unto the appointed time of God's purpose; is related to an awesome, peculiar King and Royal Priest named Melchizedek, and Christ's Resurrection DNA which has the power of an endless life (Hebrews 7:17)! Christ is the Resurrection and the Life, and the Resurrection is an order (Order of The Holy Spirit). Jesus as a forerunner into that order must be joined by heirs who will attain that order. The Resurrection is a Man. Jesus told Martha, "I AM the resurrection and I AM the life"(John 11:25). When we are transformed into His image we can have His DNA and move into this order.

# Works Cited

1. Amsden, Patti. *Portals: Releasing the Power and Presence of God into the Earth*. Collinsville: Patti Amsden Ministry, 2007.
2. Charles, R. H. *The Book of Enoch*. Eugene: Wipf & Stock Publishers, 2005.
3. Horn, Thomas. *Nephilim Stargates: The Year 2012 and The Return of the Watchers*. Crane: Anomalos Publishing House, 2007.
4. Horn, Thomas and Chris D. Putname. *Exo-Vaticana*. Crane: Defender, 2013.
5. Malone, Henry. *Portals to Cleansing*. Irving: Vision Life Publication, 2002.
6. Roberts, Scott Alan. *The Rise and Fall of the Nephilim*. Pompton Plains: Career Press Ink, 2012.
7. Strong, James. *The New Strong's Exhaustive Concordance of the Bible*. Nashville: Thomas Nelson Publishers, 2010.
8. *The American Heritage College Dictionary*. 3rd ed. Boston: Houghton Mifflin Co., 1993.
9. *The Companion Bible King James Version*. Grand Rapids: Kregel Publications, 1922.

For more information, speaking engagements, PowerPoint presentations, classes, teaching sessions, and healing and miracle ministry, contact

*Etienne M. Graves Jr.* at

<u>MEMO</u>

Melchizedek's Excellent Ministry Order

PO Box 4505

Ontario, California 91761

(323) 532-8198 e-mail: etmelchizedek@yahoo.com

Facebook: facebook.com/etiennegraves

Twitter: @etiennememo